W9-BFX-428

THE ECONOMISTS' VOICE 2.0

THE
ECONOMISTS'
VOICE 2.0

The Financial Crisis, Health Care Reform, and More

Aaron S. Edlin

Joseph E. Stiglitz

EDITORS

Bradford DeLong

William Gale

James Hines

Jeffrey Zwiebel

COEDITORS

Columbia University Press

New York

Columbia University Press
Publishers Since 1893
New York   Chichester, West Sussex
cup.columbia.edu
Copyright © 2012 Columbia University Press

Library of Congress Cataloging-in-Publication Data

The economists' voice 2.0 : the financial crisis, health care reform,
and more / editors, Aaron S. Edlin, Joseph E. Stiglitz ; coeditors,
Bradford DeLong . . . [et al.]
      p. cm.
   Includes bibliographical references and index.
   ISBN 978-0-231-16014-8 (cloth : alk. paper) —
ISBN 978-0-231-50432-4 (ebook)
    1. United States—Economic conditions—2009–   2. United States—
Economic policy—2009–   3. Economics—United States.   I. Edlin,
Aaron S.   II. Stiglitz, Joseph E.   III. DeLong, J. Bradford.
IV. Economists' voice.

   HC106.84E38 2012
   330.973—dc23   2011047626

⊛

Columbia University Press books are printed on permanent and durable
acid-free paper.

This book is printed on paper with recycled content.

Printed in the United States of America

c 10 9 8 7 6 5 4 3 2 1

References to Internet Web sites (URLs) were accurate at the time of writing.
Neither the author nor Columbia University Press is responsible for URLs
that may have expired or changed since the manuscript was prepared.

Contents

THE
ECONOMISTS'
VOICE 2.0

PART I

HEALTH CARE REFORM

CHAPTER 1

The Health Care Reform Legislation: An Overview

Chapin White

THE AFFORDABLE CARE ACT (ACA) represents the most significant overhaul of our health care system since the establishment of Medicare and Medicaid. The ACA does two things: First, it fundamentally shifts the social contract in the United States. Starting in 2014, individuals will be required to have health insurance; in return, the federal government will significantly expand low-income health insurance subsidies. Second, it significantly rebalances the financing for Medicare by reducing the growth in outlays and increasing Medicare taxes paid by high earners.

This chapter provides non-specialists with a guide to the major provisions, their logic, and the federal budgetary implications. (All revenue and spending figures that follow refer to 10-year totals for

Chapin White is a Senior Health Researcher at the Center for Studying Health System Change (HSC). He was an analyst at the Congressional Budget Office (CBO) from 2004 through 2010 and was one of the lead analysts working on the scoring of the health care reform bill. The analysis and conclusions expressed in this chapter are the author's alone and should not be interpreted as those of the CBO or HSC.

FY 2010 to 2019 and are based on CBO and Joint Tax Committee estimates.)

MEDICARE

The ACA reduces Medicare outlays by roughly $400 billion. Two-thirds of this comes from reduced growth in the payment rates that medical providers receive in the traditional fee-for-service program (see Table 1.1). Most of the rest comes from reductions in premiums paid to privately managed care plans. The payment rate reductions—roughly one percentage point a year—apply broadly to most types of medical services, except for physicians (who have no reductions) and home health care agencies (which face disproportionately large cuts).

On the revenue side, the ACA raises Medicare hospital insurance (HI) taxes by over $200 billion. Starting in 2013, earnings above a cutoff ($200,000 for singles; $250,000 for couples) will be subject to an additional 0.9 percent tax, on top of the current 2.9 percent. Also starting in 2013, high-earning families will pay a new 3.8 percent HI tax on net investment income (interest, dividends, rents, and taxable capital gains). The ACA also raises the premiums that high-income Medicare beneficiaries will pay for physician and prescription drug coverage and reduces federal subsidies to hospitals that disproportionately serve low-income patients (DSH). Also, deductibles and coinsurance in Medicare Part D prescription drug plans (the "donut hole") will shrink over the next decade, due to a combination of manufacturer discounts and additional federal financing.

The combination of reduced outlays and increased revenues substantially improves Medicare's fiscal picture and pushes the Part A insolvency date—the year in which the Medicare Trustees project that the HI trust fund will be exhausted—from 2017 to 2029. The reduction in premiums paid to Medicare Advantage will likely lead those plans to raise premiums or cut benefits, which will cause some

TABLE 1.1

Summary of the Major Provisions in the ACA

	Effect on Federal Deficit (2010–19, $ billions)
Medicare Provisions	
Reduced provider payment rates	–230
Reduced premiums to private plans	–140
Increased premiums for high-income beneficiaries	–40
Close "donut hole"	40
New HI tax on high earners	–210
Miscellaneous (DSH, IPAB, CMI, ACOs, bundling, etc.)	–50
Net, Medicare Provisions	*–610*
Coverage and Revenue Provisions	
Medicaid expansion	430
Exchange credits	460
Small business credit	40
Tax on health insurers and manufacturers	–110
Penalties on firms and individuals	–70
Limit deductibility of health care expenses	–30
Nonhealth revenue provisions	–50
High-premium excise tax	–20
Reduce Medicaid Rx prices	–40
Miscellaneous (administrative simplification, high-risk pool, early retirees, etc.)	–30
Net, Coverage and Revenue Provisions	*590*

Note: This table excludes the off-budget effects of the ACA on the Social Security program and excludes the CLASS act and the education provisions in the ACA.

beneficiaries to shift out of those plans and back to the fee-for-service program.

Rhetoric claiming that the ACA will accomplish more fundamental Medicare reform is generally overblown. For example, the new Independent Payment Advisory Board (IPAB) has been touted as the ACA's "most important institutional change." The concept was to delegate to a body outside Congress the authority to make fiscally sound, but unpopular, changes to Medicare. But IPAB is highly constrained in its design. Its reforms are limited in nature (no rationing, no restricting benefits); in scope (hospitals and most other providers are off-limits until 2019); and in timing (IPAB can only make reforms if projected Medicare-spending growth exceeds a target growth rate). Crucially, IPAB's target growth rate—GDP per capita plus one percentage point—is unsustainably high, which essentially ensures that IPAB will not solve Medicare's long-term financing problem.

Three other Medicare provisions have also received outsized attention:

- *Center for Medicare and Medicaid Innovation (CMI).* The ACA expands the executive branch's authority to conduct "demonstrations" testing alternative payment and delivery systems in Medicare and Medicaid. How the CMI will play out is highly uncertain. The CBO projected that it would have essentially no impact on spending.

- *Accountable care organizations (ACOs).* The concept behind ACOs is to encourage medical providers to form integrated systems and to incentivize those systems to reduce utilization while meeting quality benchmarks. But under the ACA, provider participation is purely voluntary, and incentives are one-sided: bonuses are available for ACOs that come in below a spending target, but there is no penalty for overshooting. Some ACOs will likely end up earning windfall bonuses due to the natural variability in health spending. The CBO guessed that, on the whole, ACOs would very modestly reduce Medicare spending, but those windfalls could very easily end up increasing it instead.

- *Bundling.* Paying medical providers for a broadly defined "bundle" of services (rather than by individual service) holds great promise for reining in cost growth. The ACA includes a bundling provision but only creates a limited pilot program for payments for hospital and post-acute care.

COVERAGE

The ACA's core coverage goals were (1) to ensure that everyone, regardless of health status or income, has adequate access to health insurance and health care; and (2) to minimize disruptions to the current system. The ACA's coverage provisions have four interdependent components: (1) subsidies for low-income individuals; (2) an individual mandate; (3) a prohibition on insurers' denying coverage or varying premiums on the basis of health status; and (4) the definition of a minimum health insurance package. Without the subsidies, health care is unaffordable for those with low incomes. Without the mandate, healthier individuals opt out of the market, possibly leading to collapse. Without the limits on insurers, market pressures force them to charge higher premiums to individuals in poor health status or deny them coverage altogether. The defined minimum benefit package is necessary to determine whether individuals have satisfied the mandate and whether they have enrolled in coverage that is eligible for the new subsidies.

Subsidies. Medicaid—which provides health care coverage with no premiums and very low or no cost sharing—has historically only been available to children in very low-income families, and their parents. Starting in 2014, the ACA will expand eligibility to every person below 138 percent of the federal poverty level (FPL) including, most importantly, adults without young children. This expansion is, in my judgment, the largest single component of the ACA. It accounts for roughly half of gross coverage costs. By 2019, it will shift roughly 16 million people into Medicaid (a number nearly as large as the number of elderly persons who enrolled in Medicare when it was first launched). For the non-elderly and non-disabled, the ACA standardizes the income-counting rules used for determining Medicaid eligibility and eliminates asset tests. Additional provisions streamline and simplify enrollment in Medicaid.

Beginning in 2014, the ACA will offer a refundable tax credit for the purchase of health insurance through newly established health insurance markets ("exchanges"). These credits (discussed in the chapter in this book by Duggan and Kocher) account for the bulk of the remainder of gross coverage costs. The ACA also includes an employer tax credit that can offset up to half of employer contributions for health insurance, but only for very small firms with low-wage workers. This credit, compared to other aspects of the ACA, is small and has relatively little impact on coverage.

Individual mandate. Also beginning in 2014, the ACA will require almost everyone in the United States to enroll in health insurance. Once fully phased in, the penalty for not doing so will equal the greater of a flat dollar amount ($695 per uninsured adult) and 2.5 percent of family income. Groups exempt from the penalty include families with income below the income-tax-filing threshold; American Indians; and families for whom the cost of coverage would be unaffordable (defined as exceeding 8 percent of income) or would result in hardship (to be defined later). The IRS will monitor compliance and assess penalties through the tax system.

Limits on insurers. In most states, health insurers in the individual market have been permitted to choose whether to offer coverage based on an individual's health history; exclude coverage for "preexisting" (i.e., already diagnosed) medical conditions; vary premiums on the basis of health status; and rescind coverage if the insurer uncovers "misstatements" (whether intentional or not) on the enrollee's application. Under the ACA, starting in 2014, all four of those practices will be prohibited in the individual insurance market. The ACA also places new restrictions on insurers in the small-employer and large-employer markets, but those restrictions are generally not binding.

Minimum coverage. The ACA defines three rings of insurance coverage: The outermost ring consists of all coverage satisfying the individual mandate. (This includes everything we would deem "real" health insurance: Medicare counts, but not, say, vision only.) The second, smaller ring consists of all small-group and individual coverage. Starting in 2014, these plans must provide "essential health benefits," which will include coverage of a broad set of services (hospital, prescription drugs, etc.), and must choose a cost-sharing design that fits into one of five actuarial value tiers ("platinum," "gold," etc.). The innermost ring consists of "qualified health plans": plans offered through the new exchanges and potentially eligible for exchange credits. These plans must be certified by the exchanges as meeting additional criteria relating to plan quality, marketing, and value.

REVENUES

To offset the cost of its subsidies, the ACA raises federal revenues from various sources, mostly within the health care system. These revenues include: broad-based taxes on health insurers and makers of brand-name prescription drugs and medical devices; penalties on large employers that do not offer affordable health coverage and on uninsured individuals; limits on the deductibility of medical expenses for individuals and firms; and some miscellaneous non-health revenue provisions (e.g., an excise tax on indoor tanning). The ACA also includes several provisions that reduce federal outlays and thereby offset some of the coverage costs, such as a reduction in the prices that Medicaid will pay for prescription drugs.

MARKETS

Several major components of the ACA attempt to correct perceived market distortions, create new markets, or improve the functioning of existing markets. Besides exchanges, discussed in the chapter by Duggan and Kocher, these changes include:

- *Limiting the tax subsidy for employer-sponsored coverage.* The tax treatment of employer-sponsored health benefits—that is, deductibility for the employer and exclusion from taxable income for the employee—has long drawn fire from economists, most notably Martin Feldstein, for putting upward pressure on health care costs. The ACA takes a small step in the direction of limiting that tax subsidy. Beginning in 2018, insurers and self-insured employers will be subject to an excise tax on employer-sponsored health benefits in excess of a ceiling. The ceiling will be at least $10,200 for single plans and $27,500 for family plans in 2018—higher if premiums grow faster than expected, if an employer's workforce is unusually old, or if the enrollee is a retiree or a worker in a high-risk profession. The ceiling, which is indexed to the Consumer Price Index-All Urban Consumers (CPI-U), will likely grow more slowly than premiums, which means that its impact is projected to grow gradually.
- *A new long-term-care insurance product.* The private market for long-term-care insurance has never really gotten off the ground due, at least in part, to the inherent instability in private insurance contracts spanning many years or decades. The ACA establishes the Community Living Assistance Services and Supports (CLASS) program, which was designed to be a voluntary, community-rated long-term-care insurance product administered by the federal government and fully funded by enrollee premiums. (In late 2011, the Administration determined that the CLASS program could not be implemented in a financially sustainable way, and the program has been discontinued.)
- *Administrative simplification.* The ACA broadens the scope of federal regulations governing interactions among health insurers and providers (e.g., submission of claims for payment, eligibility verification). The CBO judged that the resulting

reduction in premiums would be "modest" in percentage terms, but the base over which those savings accrue—almost the whole of health spending in the United States—is enormous.

- *Minimum loss ratios (MLRs).* The ACA requires, as of 2011, that health insurers spend at least a minimum percentage of their premium revenues on medical claims (i.e., losses) or quality-improvement activities. That minimum equals 80 percent in the individual and small-group markets and 85 percent in the large-group market. In the individual market, many insurers currently have loss ratios well below this cutoff, which means that their current business model and cost structure are no longer viable. It remains to be seen whether MLRs will improve the individual market or seriously disrupt it.

(The ACA contains numerous other provisions, most relating to quality improvement, public health, home-based services, and the health care workforce. They include expanded federal funding for community health centers, state-run high-risk pools, and health benefits for early retirees. They are mentioned here only in passing, as they are relatively unimportant fiscally and unrelated to the core coverage provisions.)

CONCLUSIONS

Historically, the pattern has been for the Medicare program's fiscal condition to deteriorate until—with insolvency looming—Congress temporarily rights the ship by reducing outlays and raising revenues. The ACA fits squarely in that tradition, but with a major twist: all of the Medicare savings and new revenues were spent on a major coverage expansion. The result is that Congress soon will be looking either for more Medicare savings or revenues, or for other ways to offset the cost of the coverage expansion. Either way, the policy focus will almost certainly shift rapidly from coverage to health care cost containment.

REFERENCES AND FURTHER READING

Congressional Budget Office. 2010. "H.R. 4872, Reconciliation Act of 2010 (Final Health Care Legislation)." Cost estimate for the amendment in the nature of a substitute for H.R. 4872, incorporating a proposed manager's amendment made public on March 20, 2010. Available at www.cbo.gov/doc.cfm?index=11379.

House Office of the Legislative Counsel. 2010. "Patient Protection and Affordable Care Act (ACA & HCERA; Public Laws 111–148 & 111–152: Consolidated Print)." Available at www.ncsl.org/documents /health/ppacaconsolidated.pdf.

Joint Committee on Taxation. 2010. "Estimated Revenue Effects of the Amendment in the Nature of a Substitute to H.R. 4872, the Reconciliation Act Of 2010." Amended, in combination with the revenue effects of H.R. 3590, the "Patient Protection and Affordable Care Act ('ACA')," as passed by the Senate, and scheduled for consideration by the House Committee on Rules on March 20. Available at www .jct.gov/publications.html?func=showdown&id=3672.

CHAPTER 2

The Simple Economics
of Health Reform

David M. Cutler

THE AFFORDABLE CARE ACT (ACA) is the most important piece of health care legislation since the creation of Medicare and Medicaid. The ACA[1] touches every corner of the medical system, addressing issues ranging from how people get health insurance coverage, to what type of care they receive, to how that care is paid for. Its impact will be felt for decades.

The ACA was, and is, enormously controversial. It passed without any Republican votes and with a mixture of public support and opposition. Republicans have vowed to repeal it and replace it with something smaller. Thus the ACA itself may change, even as it changes the medical system.

Full disclosure: I am a proponent of the legislation. I worked to craft President Obama's health care proposal when he ran for president

David M. Cutler is the Otto Eckstein Professor of Applied Economics in the Department of Economics and Kennedy School of Government at Harvard and a Research Associate at the National Bureau of Economic Research (NBER).

and was senior health care advisor to his campaign. I continued to advise the administration and Congress as the bill moved forward. By nature, therefore, this article will highlight more of the ACA's good features than its bad.

Two features of the ACA have particular economic salience: (1) taking steps to insure all Americans and regulating insurance companies so that can happen; and (2) reforming the financing and delivery of medical services. Here I address each issue in turn.

INSURANCE COVERAGE AND REGULATION

An estimated 47 million people in the United States lack health insurance coverage, and without reform, that figure was projected to rise to 54 million by 2019.[2] The first goal of the ACA is to extend insurance coverage to as many of those individuals as possible. Out of the projected 54 million uninsured, about 10 million will be in the country illegally. The goal of the legislation, with respect to non-citizens, was to extend coverage to uninsured legal residents. Together with U.S. citizens, the total number applicable for coverage is projected to be 44 million by the end of the decade.

Substantial empirical evidence shows that the major issues influencing insurance take-up are price and accessibility. The price elasticity for insurance is high, and people find it difficult to search for coverage on their own. To address the price issue, the ACA provides income-based subsidies to low- and middle-income individuals to purchase coverage. Families with an income below 133 percent of the federal poverty line (about $30,000 in 2010) will pay 2 percent of their income for health insurance. Subsidies phase out when an income of 400 percent of the federal poverty line (about $88,000 in 2010) is reached.

To make insurance accessible, the ACA creates a set of regional health insurance exchanges for individuals and small businesses, modeled after those operating in Massachusetts and Utah. The exchanges (discussed at greater length in the chapter in this book by Duggan and Kocher) will certify plans, collect and process contributions, ensure that insurance products are standardized, and distribute risk-adjusted payments to plans.

In many cases, the coverage provisions in the ACA match those in Massachusetts—which uses an insurance exchange and subsidizes insurance for low- and middle-income people. As a result of the subsidies and the establishment of the exchange, the share of the population in Massachusetts that is uninsured fell by three-quarters. Thus the Massachusetts experience was instrumental in convincing people that coverage could be made universal.

Insurance exchanges involve choice, but choice in insurance markets is problematic. If premiums are pooled across healthy and sick people, healthy people will find insurance less attractive and may drop out. If insurers are allowed complete pricing freedom, in contrast, they will exclude the less healthy from coverage. Selection by either individuals or insurers can thus undermine efficiency and equity goals.

To reduce selection on the part of individuals, the ACA has several features. First, it extends subsidies only to purchases made through an exchange. Effectively, this means that all non-group purchases will occur through exchanges, thus enabling transfers across individuals. Second, it allows people under age 26 to be covered on their parents' policy. Since the members of this group are the least likely to buy coverage on their own, this limits the extent of selection. Third, the ACA requires that employers with more than 200 employees automatically enroll employees into insurance plans, with opt-out disenrollment (as opposed to opt-in enrollment).

Finally, the ACA mandates that individuals either buy insurance or face a penalty of the greater of $695 per person or 2.5 percent of income. This last part of the ACA is particularly controversial, and a number of states are suing the federal government over its constitutionality. Analysts differ as to whether or not eliminating the individual mandate would materially affect insurance coverage, though a commitment to large subsidies is essential without a mandate.

Insurers are also constrained in their operations. They must underwrite everyone who wants coverage and renew coverage at the individual's option. Thus rescissions of policies to the sick are not allowed. Further, policies cannot have lifetime limits on covered services. In addition, premiums in insurance exchanges are only allowed to vary by age, smoking status, and geographic location, not by other measures of health status.

The trade-off for the insurers is that the ACA does not have a "public option"—a government-sponsored plan competing alongside and supported by many on the left as a foundation for a single-payer system, if one should be judged to be necessary down the road. For the same reason, the insurance industry vociferously opposed a public option. The compromise was strong regulation.

Two issues are central to the success of insurance reform. The first is how many people the ACA will cover. The Congressional Budget Office (CBO) estimated that 32 million uninsured persons will take up coverage, resulting in 94 percent of the eligible population having coverage. At such coverage levels, most analysts believe that residual selection is not large enough to materially affect outcomes, though others—including insurers—remain worried about an adverse-selection "death spiral."

The second issue is whether employers will drop coverage, sending more people into the exchanges. For many people, the subsidies received through the exchange are greater than the savings from the tax exclusion of employer-based health insurance available with employer-based coverage. Partly to prevent this, the ACA requires all but the smallest employers to offer coverage or pay a fee to the exchange. Interestingly, Massachusetts has seen an increase, not a decrease, in private coverage, even with a very generous set of subsidies and no employer mandate. Following this example, the CBO estimate of the ACA assumed very little dropping of employer-based insurance.

The models used by the CBO and others to estimate insurance coverage changes are not ideal. They are based on elasticities in employer-sponsored insurance settings or Medicaid, neither of which is a natural fit for new exchanges. Further, they do not account for the opt-out provisions of the law, which in other settings have had a large impact on take-up. Finally, they are extrapolated from small changes, when the ACA is much larger. For these reasons, the coverage estimates for the ACA are subject to uncertainty. It will thus be essential to monitor trends as they occur and be flexible about implementation.

THE DELIVERY OF MEDICAL SERVICES

A great deal of evidence shows that the delivery of medical care is inefficient: people pay more, and get less, from the medical system than they ought to. The inefficiency is manifested in several ways: too much care is provided in acute settings; preventive care and chronic care are not utilized to the extent they should be; and there are excess layers of administration and wasted resources. Estimates suggest that anywhere from 30 to 50 percent of medical spending is not needed to realize the outcomes we achieve—a waste of about $1 trillion annually.

The ACA attempts to rectify this. Indeed, the lengthiest sections of the ACA are those that are designed to reform the incentives of the medical system. The philosophy behind the ACA has three parts: First, the lack of good information inhibits better care. Patient information is generally not electronic, and care is based on too little evidence. A common guess is that only 10 to 20 percent of what is done in medicine is founded on a good evidence base.

Second, the lack of good information is compounded by perverse financial incentives. Providers paid on a fee-for-service or piece-rate basis do many more tests and procedures than those paid on a global basis, without any improvement in outcomes. On the flip side, services that are reimbursed only poorly, such as patient outreach, team-based consultation, and chronic care management, are underprovided, leading to too much serious disease.

Third, Medicare is the key actor in reforming payments and the use of information. Medicare accounts for 25 percent of overall medical spending, and an even larger share of acute care payments. Without Medicare reform, no payment reform can be successful. In turn, successful Medicare reform will spur changes in private insurance as well.

The first step in delivery system reform actually predates the ACA. The HITECH Act of 2009, a part of the American Recovery and Reinvestment Act, allocated $30 billion over five years to support the adoption of electronic medical records. The ACA builds on the HITECH Act to change the way that medicine is reimbursed. Specifically, the ACA has a variety of demonstrations, pilots, and new programs designed to move away from fee-for-service Medicare payments and toward a system of more "bundled" payments. For example, the ACA proposes to take all payments related to an acute event (such as a hip fracture or stroke) and group them into a single total. Providers that receive the bundled payment would then be responsible for the hospital costs, post-hospital rehabilitation, and subsequent follow-up care for those patients. Providers that limit unnecessary care (for example, reducing readmission) and seek out more efficient suppliers would make money; more wasteful ones would lose money.

This type of methodology shows up in many guises: from bundled chronic disease programs, to accountable care organizations (bundling payments for patients as a whole), to pay-for-performance programs for primary care physicians. The hope is that, within a few years, fee-for-service payment will be the residual—rather than the dominant—mode of medical care payment.

The fact that many of these new programs are demonstrations or pilots has raised some concerns. Skeptics view the plethora of programs as a wasteful commitment that is unlikely to amount to much.

The CBO, for example, judged that none of these programs would save significant sums. In reality, though, this focus on demonstrations and pilot programs reflects the fact that policy analysts did not have a strong sense about which reforms would be most successful, and what their precise contours should be. Thus the idea was to unleash a period of widespread experimentation and to build upon the successful changes.

For delivery system reform to be effective, medical care providers will need to make significant changes. Practices done on paper will need to be done electronically. Doctors who work individually will need to join teams. Hospitals that make money by doing more surgery will have to figure out how to become more efficient.

Whether this will occur, and at what speed it will happen, is the major unknown about health care reform. Again, flexibility will be key. During this period of experimentation, the federal government, as well as providers themselves, will need to evaluate continuously and change liberally. For much of American business, experimentation has become the norm—but not in medical care. It will certainly be a culture shock, but it is one other industries have absorbed.

THE BIG QUESTIONS

There is much more to the ACA than these two areas. Insurance coverage is expensive in the short run, so money is raised from higher-income people, and Medicare and Medicaid costs are reduced. Money is spent to research the quality of different medical care providers. Payments to primary care providers are increased, and additional opportunities are created for preventive care. A Prevention and Public Health Fund is set up to fund programs in those areas.

All of these are important changes, but they are dwarfed by the coverage, insurance market, and delivery system reforms. Put simply, health care reform will succeed or fail based on two fundamental criteria: Do people get the coverage that they were promised, and that they want? And, do we change the delivery of medicine to promote high-quality, lower-cost care? If the answer to these questions is yes, the ACA will turn out to be the most successful piece of health care legislation ever, not just the largest one.

NOTES

1. For a detailed description of the ACA's provisions, see www.kff .org/healthreform/upload/8061.pdf.

2. For details of the insurance and federal budget calculations from the Congressional Budget Office (CBO), see www.cbo.gov/ftpdocs/113xx /doc11379/AmendReconProp.pdf.

CHAPTER 3

The Economics, Opportunities, and Challenges of Health Insurance Exchanges

Mark G. Duggan and Robert Kocher

A CENTRAL COMPONENT of the Affordable Care Act (ACA) is the creation of state-based health insurance exchanges, which have the potential to substantially improve the functioning and expand the reach of the private health insurance market. Here we describe salient features of the current market for health insurance and explain how the exchanges will build on this system by altering incentives for individuals, employers, and insurers. We conclude with a discussion of the challenges and key issues that remain.

Mark G. Duggan is Professor of Economics at the University of Maryland, a Research Associate at the National Bureau of Economic Research, and former Senior Economist for Health Care Policy, Council of Economic Advisers.

Robert Kocher, MD, is Partner at Venrock Associates, a Non-Resident Senior Fellow, Brookings Institution, and former Special Assistant to the President for Health Care and Economic Policy, National Economic Council.

THE PRIVATE HEALTH INSURANCE MARKET

The U.S. private health insurance market has been dominated by employer-sponsored insurance (ESI). In 2009, more than 90 percent of the 172 million non-elderly individuals with private health insurance obtained it through their, or a family member's, employer (U.S. Census Bureau 2010). The dominance of ESI is due to the tax subsidy for employer-provided health insurance, the benefits of pooling together many individuals when negotiating contracts with health insurers, and other factors.

The system, however, works relatively poorly for employees of small firms. Small firms are much less likely to offer insurance, are likely to offer fewer plan options when they do, and must pay up to 18 percent more than their larger counterparts for the same policy. While 98 percent of firms with 200 or more employees offered ESI to their workers in 2009, just 46 percent of firms with three to nine employees did (Kaiser Family Foundation and Health Research and Educational Trust [hereafter KFF] 2009). As a result, employees of small firms (and their dependents) are significantly more likely than workers at large firms to lack health insurance. The problems are similar for the self-employed and even more pronounced for those who are not working.

Individuals without ESI coverage can buy private health insurance on the individual market, though without the tax subsidy ESI enjoys. Partly because of the resulting higher (net) prices, individual policies tend to be much less comprehensive than ESI policies. Additionally, individuals with existing health problems often find it difficult or impossible to obtain coverage at affordable rates. Moreover, it is difficult for individuals to conduct "apples-to-apples" comparisons of the price and quality of available plan options. Partly because of this, the individual market is thin, insuring just 6 percent of non-elderly individuals in 2009.

From 1999 to 2009, average ESI premiums increased by 70 percent in real terms, while median household income (which excludes employer contributions for ESI) actually *declined* by 5 percent. Largely because of this contrast, private health insurance coverage fell to 65 percent of the non-elderly population, versus what had been 74 percent ten years earlier.

THE EXCHANGES

The ACA will increase health insurance coverage beginning in January 2014, through two channels: First, Medicaid eligibility will be extended to individuals with incomes up to 133 percent of the federal poverty line (FPL). While current income thresholds for Medicaid eligibility vary widely across states, this is an expansion for almost all states. For example, 40 states currently have Medicaid eligibility thresholds below 133 percent of FPL for low-income parents, with the median state having a threshold of 64 percent and the lowest, Arkansas, just 17 percent. Eligibility standards are even tighter for childless adults, with just six states providing any Medicaid coverage for this group (KFF 2009).

Second, the creation of state-based health insurance exchanges will allow individuals to select from qualified health plans operating in their area of residence. By 2019, the new rules will raise Medicaid enrollment by 16 million, and the exchanges will cover an additional 24 million people. When these changes are combined with an expected 8 million-person decline in the number of people with other sources of private coverage, the ACA will reduce the number of uninsured people by a total of 32 million (CBO 2010).

Individuals without an affordable ESI offer will be able to acquire coverage through the exchanges, with subsidies that decline with income available for households with incomes between 133 percent and 400 percent of FPL. The subsidies are structured so that individuals with higher incomes receive smaller subsidies. (For example, a family of four with a 2014 income of $45,000 receives a subsidy of $9,500 to purchase a $12,100 family policy, while a similar family with an income of $90,000 would receive approximately $3,600.) Additionally, firms with up to 100 workers will be able to acquire coverage for their workers through the exchanges, although their workers would not be eligible for the premium subsidies.

The ACA requires states to set up exchanges by January 2014, but it gives them considerable latitude as to structure. A state can set up one exchange that serves both individuals and small employers, or it can segment these markets with separate exchanges. Similarly, states can join together to form regional exchanges, which are likely to be relatively attractive to states with low populations, in order to stabilize risk pools and premium fluctuations. Perhaps most noteworthy, beginning in 2017, states can allow firms with more than 100 workers to acquire coverage for their workers through the exchanges.

Key Functions of the Exchanges

In practice, state exchanges will have five primary functions:

1. determine which plans can be offered
2. assist consumers in choosing between plans based on price and quality
3. determine subsidies for which individuals are eligible, and calculate net premiums
4. minimize incentives for plans to preferentially target particular segments of individuals and employers
5. perform risk adjustments to mitigate plans' cherry-picking profitable consumers

How exchanges operationalize these functions will largely determine how successfully the exchange market functions. Implementing each function will require skillful trade-offs. For example, effective competition and shopping can be achieved by having several plan options without overwhelming consumers with choice. Today, most individuals and small groups do not have sufficient choice to enable effective shopping. On the opposite extreme, many workers in the Federal Employees Health Benefits (FEHB) Program have too many choices, leading to the majority of workers' aggregating to a single plan and resulting in ineffective competition since the FEHB Program does not give consumers adequate information to clarify the trade-offs across plans.

If exchanges commoditize plan offering to enable simple price-comparison shopping for consumers, the result could be exchanges precluding plans from offering innovative benefit designs such as narrow provider networks and large incentives for preventive care that are important approaches for constraining premium growth. When it comes to subsidy determination, the frequency with which income data are updated (e.g., quarterly, annually) will affect the inevitable shifting of people between Medicaid and the exchange and will affect future tax obligations for those whose incomes increase (and, thus, whose subsidies decrease) mid-year.

Additionally, there is the question of how effectively exchanges reduce distortions resulting from premiums that are constrained by rating rules that limit variation to 3:1 based on age, with adjustments only for smoking status. The level of effectiveness here will be critical in ensuring competition across the entirety of the exchange. Certain groups, such as young people who smoke, could be disproportionately profitable, since they will have high premiums relative to their expected costs. In contrast, older non-smokers may have artificially low premiums and could be unprofitable. Additionally, exchanges will have to risk adjust plan payments so that plans attracting a disproportionate share of sicker patients will not be penalized. However, the federal government's recent experience with payments to Medicare Advantage plans suggests that this will be very difficult.

Economic Benefits of the Exchanges

Effective exchanges will bring millions of people into the market for private health insurance through the mandate and the sliding-scale subsidies. For small businesses, one major benefit of exchanges could be disintermediating brokers and their commissions—which can equal as much as 10 percent of the premium. Moreover, small businesses gain far greater premium stability by being a part of a larger risk pool with the new rating rules.

Also, the exchanges will provide a powerful incentive for insurers to price competitively, since individuals will bear the full cost on the margin of more generous plans. In contrast, workers who purchase insurance through employers today are shielded from the full marginal cost, partly because of the tax exclusion. In response, plans are likely to innovate in ways that reduce premium growth by increasing the productivity of their provider networks and the effectiveness of medical-management programs—not just by trying to drive unit prices down.

Potential Weaknesses of the Exchanges

To deliver the consumer and economic benefits of exchanges, operators must overcome two potential policy shortcomings: First, setting exchanges at the level of the state was largely a political choice, not an economic one. While this choice allows states flexibility to tailor plan choices to the needs of their residents—perhaps fostering new entrants and allowing local plans to participate—it makes it far harder to achieve scale and consistency for key functions.

Moreover, it significantly complicates preparations for the 2014 launch. (Simply getting IT systems for subsidy determination and Medicaid eligibility to work in each state will be a major accomplishment, let alone constructing a risk-adjustment algorithm and determining how many plans are eligible.) Since many states have small populations, risk pools will be less stable there, leading to greater premium volatility and, if premiums rise more than anticipated, greater subsidy cost.

A second major potential weakness of the ACA is that it requires separate individual and small-employer exchanges—which amplifies the volatility of small-risk pools and leads to potentially higher premiums. If premiums rise, the problem could spiral, as employers with younger and healthier workforces forgo exchanges, since they are able to obtain cheaper insurance elsewhere.

The individual market outside of exchanges is likely to wither over time, since individual subsidies can only be accessed in the exchange. In contrast, the small-group market could persist for a long time. Bifurcated markets will make avoiding adverse selection in exchanges difficult. This was the unfortunate outcome for most prior exchanges targeting businesses—most recently, the exchange run by the Pacific Business Group on Health. Also, more employers may drop coverage, since purchasing as an employer brings no benefits to a worker who can buy cheaper subsidized insurance on the individual exchange. This is particularly true for small firms that incur no penalty if they drop coverage. If this scenario becomes reality, or if the individual exchange proves to be a lower-cost and more efficient market, then the problem of employers that drop coverage could be much worse than the CBO forecast predicts.

Key Issues/Challenges for the Exchanges

The exchanges must overcome two major near-term challenges: First, the consumer experience has to work well if the ACA is to fulfill its intention of bringing in millions of uninsured (and, particularly, young and healthy) individuals. Subsidies must be accurate. Real-time shopping experiences must be intuitive and quick. Interactions should be personalized over time by medical statuses and preferences. Many private-sector firms, but few in the public sector (think of state

Medicaid or DMV offices), have shown they can deliver such experiences. Yet poor service could lead to low uptake and adverse selection. Here, well-designed sites such as healthcare.gov offer glimmers of hope, and much can be learned from examples such as the Part D plan finder and the Massachusetts Connector.

Second, risk-adjustment and product standards need to ensure that individuals in all segments of the market receive attractive insurance options. It would be unfortunate if exchanges were to give plans an incentive to target "profitable" young smokers at the expense of older and sicker individuals. The tools of branding, marketing, and product design give plans a big advantage over current risk-adjustment approaches. There is little time to develop better approaches, and the ACA only calls for prospective—not retrospective—risk adjustment. A vibrant market develops across all segments in the exchange only if each offers profit potential. To achieve this, exchanges will have to get risk adjustment to work as effectively as possible and achieve the proper balance between innovative benefit-designs and standardized plans.

CONCLUSION

How well exchanges operationalize their five key functions and how effectively they overcome these challenges will likely determine whether Americans perceive the ACA as beneficial and what will be the long-term role for exchanges as a public-policy solution. If exchanges execute their primary functions skillfully and arrive at effective solutions to these challenges, the benefits to consumers and employers will be substantial: Exchanges could serve as a catalyst that drives down premium growth, as plans seek to attract larger shares of increasingly value-conscious consumers. Moreover, by reducing distribution costs and shifting the basis of competition from underwriting to medical value, exchanges could be an instigator of significant productivity among plans and the health care sector.

Time will tell if exchanges live up to their promise. To do so will require exceptional leadership at the state level, timely federal policy, sufficient funding, and enough political inoculation to make the economic trade-offs that are necessary.

REFERENCES AND FURTHER READING

Congressional Budget Office (CBO). 2010. "H.R. 4872, Reconciliation Act of 2010 (Final Health Care Legislation)." Cost estimate for the amendment in the nature of a substitute for H.R. 4872, incorporating a proposed manager's amendment made public on March 20, 2010. Available at www.cbo.gov/doc.cfm?index=11379.

Kaiser Family Foundation (KFF) and Health Research and Educational Trust. 2009. "Employer Health Benefits: 2009 Annual Survey." Available at http://ehbs.kff.org/pdf/2009/7936.pdf.

U.S. Census Bureau. 2010. "Income, Poverty, and Health Insurance Coverage in the United States: 2009." Available at www.census.gov /prod/2009pubs/p60–236.pdf.

CHAPTER 4

Can the ACA Improve Population Health?

Dana P. Goldman and Darius N. Lakdawalla

HEALTH CARE REFORM may accomplish a number of different objectives—most notably that of providing valuable financial protection. However, its impact on population health is likely to be quite modest.

Consider the evidence: Many of the greatest improvements in health during the last century had little to do with the health care system. Clean water, public sanitation, and reduced smoking all reflect public health interventions that had dramatic benefits.

Cardiovascular disease also provides an example that yields significant insights. Between 1980 and 2000, the death rate for coronary heart disease was cut in half.[1] But only about half of this reduction came from better medical therapies. The rest—caused by lower blood

Dana P. Goldman is a Professor and the Norman Topping Chair in Medicine and Public Policy at the University of Southern California.

Darius N. Lakdawalla is the Director of Research at the Leonard Schaeffer Center for Health Policy and Economics and Associate Professor in the School of Policy, Planning, and Development at the University of Southern California.

pressure, lower cholesterol, less smoking, and other factors—came from healthier behavior and some drugs. And the treatment of heart disease is one of our greatest success stories. Our accomplishments in diabetes, cancer, and lung disease are not nearly as impressive.

Thus good health has only been partially a story about excellent health care. And that remains true today.

PROPONENTS OF THE ACA MAY BE PROMISING TOO MUCH HEALTH IMPROVEMENT

One reason health care reform proposals always seem to fail is that proponents promise too much. Reformers declare they will improve quality, lower costs, and increase access—all at the same time. This mantra is repeated so often—on both sides of the ideological divide—that the public tends to believe that it is possible, when it really isn't.

Advocates of universal coverage often get confused on this point. They equate good health with having health insurance and cite myriad academic studies. The problem is that these studies don't account for all the other differences between the insured and uninsured—what they eat, where they live, whether they smoke or drink, the amount of stress in their lives, and even their genetic predisposition to disease. No health care system is good enough to fully compensate for bad behavior and poor environmental factors.

Perhaps the strongest and earliest such evidence came from the RAND Health Insurance Experiment (HIE), which randomly assigned families to health insurance plans of varying generosity.[2] One of the main findings of this experiment was that families in the least generous plan (95 percent coinsurance) spent nearly 30 percent less on medical care—with little or no difference in their health.

Numerous other studies—such as the work of the Dartmouth group on regional variation in the use of medical care—have found, similarly, that greater utilization is not associated with better health outcomes in the traditional Medicare system. Elliot Fisher and his colleagues have demonstrated that end-of-life spending by Medicare beneficiaries varies widely across regions. Enrollees in higher-spending regions receive more care but do not appear to live longer or otherwise experience better health outcomes.

And these conclusions do not just apply to the elderly: Baicker, Buckles, and Chandra (2006) find similar results for the use of caesarean sections across counties—areas with high use (and, presumably, high spending) perform more C-sections on healthy mothers and yet enjoy no beneficial effects on either maternal or neonatal mortality.

WHEN DOES INSURANCE MATTER? WHEN IT AFFECTS COMPLIANCE WITH HIGHLY EFFECTIVE THERAPY

So when does insurance matter? Many studies examine the insured and uninsured populations and find much worse health among the uninsured. But this evidence confounds health insurance with numerous other factors——including worse health behavior, environmental risk factors, and social stressors.

The HIE examined many medical outcome measures in various subgroups of enrollees. Although it did not find compelling evidence to show that higher cost sharing led to worse health outcomes, low-income participants who were in poor health appeared to be more vulnerable to adverse outcomes. For example, poor people with high blood pressure had slightly higher mortality rates if they had high co-payments. In addition, the HIE found that participants in the high co-payment group were as likely to reduce "appropriate" as "inappropriate" care, as defined by groups of medical experts. These findings mirror the evidence from the most careful studies in this area.[3]

Of course, the HIE was conducted in the 1970s, and medicine has advanced since then. Better, but more costly, drugs for heart disease,

cancer, mental illness, and other diseases are available, but these require patients to pay more money out-of-pocket. The result is that
people do not take their medication. The impact of high prices on
patient compliance is important because poor compliance can lead to
worse health outcomes through uncontrolled hypertension, high
cholesterol, untreated psychiatric illness, and resistant bacterial in-
fection, to name a few of the relevant conditions. But non-compliance
is particularly unfortunate: not only can it worsen patient health, but
it can reduce productivity and significantly increase medical costs
as well.[4]

With a growing elderly population—and a larger baby boom gen-
eration approaching retirement—the prevalence of chronic diseases
will rise. If current trends continue, health care costs will consume an
ever-increasing share of national income. The future liability of the
Medicare program alone is estimated to be $24 trillion over the next
75 years, absent any policy changes.

HOW CAN WE TRULY IMPROVE POPULATION HEALTH? INVESTMENTS IN EDUCATION AND PREVENTION

So what can we do to more significantly improve population health?

The first step is to invest—not in the health care system but in
education. We should take the $120 billion it might cost for universal
coverage and use it instead to provide earlier education and to improve the quality of education. Better-educated people live longer, are
less likely to be disabled, and engage in healthier behavior. For nearly
40 years, distinguished health economists led by Michael Grossman
have observed that more educated people have much more powerful
incentives to protect their own "investments" in education by prac-
ticing healthier habits and reducing their risk of death.[5] They also
are better at self-managing chronic diseases.[6] And, unlike universal

coverage, more education has other valuable benefits to a person and to society: less crime, less divorce, and higher earnings—can universal health insurance promise that?

The second place to invest is in prevention. Primary prevention has the capacity to slow or reduce the rising prevalence of chronic disease and simultaneously attenuate the downstream spending that is associated with it. Equally important, however, prevention leads to a life with less disability and more years of an active lifestyle. It simply makes a lot of sense to avoid disease in the first place rather than try to treat it later.

THE ECONOMIC ARGUMENTS FOR A GOVERNMENT DISEASE-PREVENTION ROLE

There are also sound economic arguments for a strong government role in the prevention of disease. Because the benefits of prevention often accrue decades later—long after someone has switched employers or health plans—private plans will skimp on prevention coverage. The government needs to step in to fill this void. Medicare could save itself money, for example, by paying for anti-hypertensive medication before people turn 65.

Perhaps most strikingly, my colleagues and I estimate that if we could roll back obesity to levels seen in the 1980s, we could save up to hundreds of billions of dollars. We need to find a way to make this happen. One way may involve better medicine—an obesity pill would be a good start—but it may involve other methods that have little to do with health care. Maybe solutions could include an extra hour of physical education at school, or subsidized treadmills in the workplace, or even pedometers for all Americans. Clearly there would be huge returns for society on a substantial investment in combating obesity.

WHAT THE TREATMENT OF HYPERTENSION CAN TEACH
US ABOUT THE TREATMENT OF OBESITY—AND ABOUT
TREATMENT GENERALLY

Too many policy makers and researchers view medical care and medical technology as the first and only line of defense against illness. In fact, medical care has always functioned as a safety net, both for the unlucky and for those without the means or the incentives to protect themselves against the risk of illness.

The treatment of hypertension provides an instructive example. In the 1960s, primary-care physicians would instruct their hypertensive patients to manage their diet and exercise regimens to avoid worsening their disease. While this counsel is accurate, it is also difficult for many patients—particularly the least educated—to comply with. Thus the era of "behavioral" treatments for hypertension saw wide disparities in the health outcomes of more-educated and less-educated hypertensives. The arrival of beta-blockers in the 1970s changed the nature of hypertension treatment. Instead of employing a vigilant and sophisticated approach to monitoring their diet and exercise, hypertensive patients could instead take an oral medication to control their disease. The result was a dramatic increase in health outcomes for the least-educated hypertensive patients, relative to their better-educated peers. Fifteen years after the arrival of beta-blockers, virtually no disparities across education remained among hypertensive patients.[7]

This is not to say, of course, that medical technology is a blanket remedy that eliminates the value of education. A host of important diseases continues to wait for a breakthrough to supplant behavioral treatment. Obesity treatment is today's equivalent of 1960s hypertension treatment: few effective medical treatments exist for the vast majority of patients suffering from obesity or being overweight. While dietary restriction and regular exercise are proven weight-loss strategies, they rarely lead to long-term solutions for the growing proportion of American adults who are obese. And, not surprisingly, the less educated are heavier and more likely to be obese than the more educated.[8]

Moreover, obesity is not the only disease for which complex treatment regimens are the norm. Diabetes also requires sophisticated self-monitoring and adjustment—as does HIV. As a society, we can wait for breakthroughs to simplify the treatment of these conditions for the least educated, or we can invest in education in order to provide more Americans with the means and the incentives to control their weight or otherwise manage their own health. Prevention investments complement this strategy by identifying opportunities to intervene with disadvantaged populations whose schooling has long ago been completed.

Hypertension is but one example of an area in which all patients can benefit from cheap and simple therapeutic options that forestall complications. The use of aspirin for the primary prevention of cardiovascular events in high-risk adults is another.[9] Education lays the groundwork for improved health behavior by future generations; prevention can help mitigate the omissions of the past. Now that we have covered the uninsured, it is time for us to put the priority on health, not on health insurance.

NOTES

1. See Ford et al. 2007.
2. See Newhouse and T. I. E. Group 1993, 489.
3. See Levy and Meltzer 2002.
4. See Goldman and Smith 2002.
5. See Grossman 1972.
6. See Goldman and Smith 2002.
7. See Goldman and Lakdawalla 2005.
8. See Lakdawalla and Philipson 2009.
9. See Wolff, Miller, and Ko 2009.

REFERENCES AND FURTHER READING

Baicker, K., K. S. Buckles, and A. Chandra. 2006. "Geographic Variation in the Appropriate Use of Cesarean Delivery." *Health Affairs* 25, no. 5: w355–67. Available at http://content.healthaffairs.org/cgi/content /abstract/25/5/w355.

Fisher, E. S., et al. 2003. "The Implications of Regional Variations in Medicare Spending. Part 2: Health Outcomes and Satisfaction with Care." *Annals of Internal Medicine* 138, no. 4: 288–98. Available at www.annals.org/content/138/4/288.abstract.

Ford, E. S., et al. 2007. "Explaining the Decrease in U.S. Deaths from Coronary Disease, 1980–2000." *New England Journal of Medicine* 356, no. 23: 2388–98. Available at www.nejm.org/doi/full/10.1056/NEJM sa053935.

Goldman, D. P., G. F. Joyce, and Y. Zheng. 2007. "Prescription Drug Cost Sharing: Associations with Medication and Medical Utilization and Spending and Health." *JAMA* 298, no. 1: 61–69. Available at http://jama.ama-assn.org/cgi/content/abstract/298/1/61.

Goldman, D. P., and D. N. Lakdawalla. 2005. "A Theory of Health Disparities and Medical Technology." *B. E. Journals in Economic Analysis and Policy* 4, no. 1: 1–30. Available at www.bepress.com/bejeap/contri butions/vol4/iss1/art8.

Goldman, D. P., and J. P. Smith. 2002. "Can Patient Self-Management Help Explain the SES Health Gradient?" *Proceedings of the National Academy of Science* 99, no. 16: 10929–34. Available at www.jstor.org /stable/3059493.

Grossman, M. 1972. "On the Concept of Health Capital and the Demand for Health." *Journal of Political Economy* 80, no. 2: 223–55. Available at www.jstor.org/stable/1830580.

Lakdawalla, D., and T. Philipson. 2009. "The Growth of Obesity and Technological Change. Economics and Human Biology." *Economics and Human Biology* 7, no. 3: 283–93. Available at www.nber.org/papers /w8946.

Levy, H., and D. O. Meltzer. 2002. "What Do We Really Know About Whether Health Insurance Affects Health?" *Annual Review of Public Health* 29: 399–409. Available at www.annualreviews.org/doi/abs/10 .1146/annurev.publhealth.28.021406.144042.

Newhouse, J. P., and T. I. E. Group. 1993. *Free for All? Lessons from the RAND Health Insurance Experiment.* Cambridge and London: Harvard University Press.

Wolff, T., T. Miller, and S. Ko. 2009. "Aspirin for the Primary Prevention of Cardiovascular Events: An Update of the Evidence for the U.S. Preventive Services Task Force." *Annals of Internal Medicine* 150, no. 6: 405–10. Available at www.annals.org/content/150/6/405.full.

CHAPTER 5

Systemic Reform of Health Care Delivery and Payment

Henry J. Aaron

THE AFFORDABLE CARE ACT (ACA) became law on March 23, 2010, but little of it is yet actively in effect. Not until January 1, 2014, will the Medicaid extensions, the individual mandate to buy insurance, the state-managed health exchanges, and the subsidies to make insurance affordable take effect. The tax on high-premium plans will not be imposed until 2018. Tight restrictions on the operations of the Independent Medicare Advisory Board will remain until 2018.

Before those dates, the law will have to clear four hurdles. The odds that it will emerge unscathed are small. It is important to understand those obstacles and to consider how they may change the reform or even prevent it from taking effect.

The first hurdle is judicial. Several states are challenging the constitutionality of the individual mandate—the requirement that everyone

Henry J. Aaron is the Bruce and Virginia MacLaury Senior Fellow at the Brookings Institution. The views expressed here are his own and do not necessarily reflect those of the trustees, officers, or other staff of Brookings.

(with a few exceptions) who is not insured at work or covered by a public program must personally buy health insurance. Scholars are divided on whether the Constitution empowers the federal government to impose such a requirement. The courts will decide.

If the individual mandate is unconstitutional and Congress puts nothing in its place, actual adverse selection, or the fear of adverse selection, would render key elements of the ACA unenforceable. The law bars insurance companies from refusing coverage to anyone. It establishes bands within which premiums must be set. And it bans insurers from cancelling coverage for those who have insurance. All three of these provisions would become unsustainable if the courts were to throw out the individual mandate. Without the mandate, people could wait to buy coverage until they became ill. How many would do so is unclear, given the subsidies available under the law to most families and individuals. But insurers would have to set prices to protect themselves against the possibility that many would "go bare" until illness strikes. They would have to set premiums high enough to cover the costs of covering the sick. A dynamic, known as a "death spiral," could occur, in which ever-higher premiums would make insurance unattractive to all but an increasingly narrow group of increasingly sick people. Or the insurers could simply stop selling health insurance. Thus the insurance market reforms hinge on the constitutionality of the individual mandate—or on an alternative incentive that is sufficiently powerful to maintain the risk pool.

Second, Republicans have sworn to seek repeal of the ACA. Doing so while President Obama remains in office is improbable. However, the election of a declared opponent to the ACA in the 2012 elections would leave a full year for repeal of much of the law. For that reason, the question of repeal will remain alive at least until the 2012 elections. In that election, Republicans may well win control of the Senate, as twenty-one Democratic senators (plus two Independents who caucus with them), but only ten Republicans, will be up for reelection. Should the economic recovery proceed as sluggishly as current forecasts indicate it will, then the Republicans' chances of winning the presidency will also be quite good. Repeal of all or major parts of the bill or substantial revision would then become possible, if not likely.

The third challenge confronting the bill is implementation. The technical challenges of implementation are enormous. For example, many observers believe that health insurance subsidies should be based on data that are more current than the tax information currently available to the IRS. Collecting such data, processing the information, paying out subsidies, and recovering overpayments are daunting tasks. Implementation also faces major political obstacles. The ACA contains 115 specific or general authorizations to spend money for various purposes. Before expenditures can be made, however, Congress must appropriate funds under each of these authorizations. In addition, the ACA appropriated $1 billion for implementation, but this sum is only a small fraction of the $5–10 billion that the Congressional Budget Office estimates will be necessary to carry out the bill. Congress could stall the bill by failing to appropriate these funds. Congressional opponents could also stall the bill by refusing to appropriate the authorized funds. Equally effective would be language in appropriation bills forbidding the expenditure of funds for specified purposes, necessary to implement the bill. (Such purposes might include hiring staff or purchasing computers to collect and process information that is needed for the payment of subsidies or for the enforcement of specific provisions, such as the mandate that businesses provide insurance to their employees.) Bills might also include language barring federal employees from processing state applications for grants under the ACA. Given the balance of political forces, tough fights lie ahead.

The fourth group of obstacles is found in state capitals. The ACA requires each of the fifty states to set up health insurance exchanges. It grants the states wide discretion as to how to organize the exchanges and where to place them in the state governmental structure. The ACA provides initial funding for the exchanges. After a brief period, however, each state will be responsible for the costs of operating the exchanges. Together with state agencies responsible for regulating health insurance, the exchanges will set the rules under which individuals and small groups buy insurance through the exchanges or outside of them. How well the states do this job is of critical importance. Insurers will be tempted to try to dump high-cost patients in the exchanges. If they succeed, premiums charged in the exchanges will be very high, rendering insurance through the exchanges burdensome or unaffordable for many people (Jost 2010). Many governors, attorneys general, and state legislators oppose the ACA. Some are party to the litigation alleging that the requirement that individuals carry insurance is unconstitutional. Should a state fail to set up an exchange or run it adequately, the ACA authorizes the federal Department of Health and Human Services to step in and perform the functions that the exchange is supposed to perform. However, the law cannot specify just what constitutes nonperformance. The risk, therefore, is that some governors or state legislatures, opposed to the bill as a whole, may create marginally effective insurance exchanges, providing them with enough money and staff to prevent federal preemption but not enough for them to operate effectively.

Should the mandate requiring individuals to carry health insurance be declared unconstitutional, much of the rest of the bill would become unsustainable, unless some alternative mechanism to create a sustainable risk pool were to be found. Various alternatives could work. Paul Starr has suggested that people who refuse each year to buy insurance should be barred for an extended period—say, four years—from buying insurance in the regulated market and from qualifying for income-related subsidies. The German health system uses such an arrangement and achieves near-universality. The answer to the question whether such a penalty could be adopted in the United States is not obvious. Nor is it clear how well such a penalty would work in the United States. Uninsured Americans would be able, as now, to show up at emergency room doors if they are seriously ill, because federal law requires that hospitals provide them services. The subsidies in the ACA might well tip the balance for most in favor of buying insurance. Such a provision would not have to work perfectly, just well enough to prevent the collapse of the health insurance pool.

Were the individual mandate to be declared unconstitutional, enacting some replacement would doubtless open up the whole bill to amendment. Approval of a time-limited exclusion from subsidized coverage or any other mechanism to maintain a risk pool would require sixty votes in a badly fractured Senate and approval by a majority in a House of Representatives now controlled by a party that has pledged to repeal the law. Opponents of the law would be disinclined to agree to provisions that sustain it; at a minimum, their price for accepting such amendments would be high.

The possible denial of funding for implementation and the possible inclusion of restrictive language raise so many possibilities that it is not possible to explore them all. The administration might manage to cobble together sufficient resources or staff from other appropriations to move implementation planning ahead, but delays would be likely. Whole provisions could be blocked. A few examples, chosen almost at random, include demonstration projects to test global payments covering the treatment of all services for particular conditions (section 2705); accountable care organizations of pediatric care (section 2706); grants or contracts for the development of measures of quality (section 3013); support of trauma care centers (section 3505); and funds to establish a prevention and public health fund (section 4002). In brief, Congress can effectively repeal much of the bill simply by failing to appropriate "such funds as are necessary" or the sums specifically authorized in the ACA.

The risks posed by failure to create viable state health insurance exchanges are less obvious than those described so far but equally serious. Even with the best of will, state legislatures face difficult challenges in designing health insurance exchanges. To make competition among health insurance plans work, exchanges will have to design a limited number of insurance models so that people are not overwhelmed by complex variations that are impossible to understand. The exchanges must design descriptive and evaluative information and present it so that customers can understand their options. States must regulate the sale of insurance both within and outside of the exchanges (or bring all insurance under the exchanges) in ways that avoid adverse selection. And they must discourage insurers from incurring high administrative costs through needless selling expenses. Success in avoiding competition via risk selection will hinge on the development of an adequate risk-adjustment system under which premiums will be allocated among insurers based on the risk profiles of enrollees. If exchanges are inadequately funded or staffed, the promised improvement in the efficiency of the small-group and individual insurance market will remain unrealized.

As things now stand, the future of the ACA is highly uncertain. Yet its success is of critical national importance. The reason, paradoxically, is the promise of the very provisions that have been subject to most criticism—those related to cost control. Quite apart from the bill's extension of coverage to nearly all legal residents, the ACA is the instrument now at hand to control the growth of health care spending, the principal driver behind projections of growing federal budget deficits. To be sure, the ACA does disappointingly little to curb the tax advantages associated with employer-financed health insurance, a failing deplored by virtually every economist, Republican or Democratic. Apart from this serious failing, however, the bill contains, at least in embryonic form, virtually every idea for cost control that any analyst has come up with:

- The bill retains health savings accounts.
- It adds pilots and demonstration programs to develop accountable care organizations and medical homes.

- It contains provisions to test the practicality of bundled payments and to develop value-based health insurance.
- It contains additional funding for comparative-effectiveness research. It spurs the introduction of health information technology.
- It directly curbs growth of Medicare spending and establishes a commission to recommend further reforms (although the commission's powers are undesirably limited).
- It contains a significant expansion of preventive care, although the cost-reducing potential of preventive care is often greatly exaggerated (Mongan, Ferris, and Lee 2008).

This menu includes all available ideas on how to control the growth of health care spending within the next few years. The most practical cost-control strategy that is now available to Congress is to accelerate the implementation of these provisions, not to stymie them.

REFERENCES AND FURTHER READING

Jost, Timothy Stoltzfus. 2010. "Health Insurance Exchanges and the Affordable Care Act: Eight Difficult Issues." Commonwealth Fund, Publication No. 144, September. Available at www.commonwealth fund.org/Content/Publications/Fund-Reports/2010/Sep/Health -Insurance-Exchanges-and-the-Affordable-Care-Act.aspx.

Mongan, James J., Timothy G. Ferris, and Thomas H. Lee. 2008. "Options for Slowing the Growth of Health Care Costs." *New England Journal of Medicine* 358: 1509–14. Available at www.nejm.org/doi/full /10.1056/NEJMsb0707912.

CHAPTER 6

How Stable Are Insurance Subsidies in Health Reform?

Mark V. Pauly

UNDER THE NEW health reforms, changes in subsidies and regulations for health insurance are now, as the phrase goes, the "law of the
land," but the stability and eventual form of this program are still far
from assured. In this chapter I want to take a step back from the details of the legislation, its political course, and its implementation to
address the question of whether key features dealing with subsidies
intended to reduce the number of uninsured people are likely to
represent a stable political equilibrium. I do not imagine that either
economists or political scientists can provide definitive predictions
about politics, and I do not intend to dig into what public opinion
polls may show. Nor will I deal with the possibility of total repeal. But
I do think it is possible to identify parts of the program that may especially call for rethinking, or at least discussion (given the small amount

Mark V. Pauly is Bendheim Professor in the Department of Health Care Management, Professor of Health Care Management, Insurance and Risk Management,
and Business and Public Policy at The Wharton School, and Professor of Economics
in the School of Arts and Sciences at the University of Pennsylvania.

of genuine legislative debate that surrounded the construction and passage of legislation that avoided bicameral conference committees). Perhaps, despite the absence of early signs, eventually voters and tax-payers will come to favor the current form of the law, but it may be useful to plan for the alternative and develop some concepts and obser-vations about how to improve the political stability of health reform.

I am going to assume that the primary goal of reform was to substantially reduce the proportion of the population without health insurance, public or private. Other goals, such as cost containment or quality improvement for the insured, Medicare reform, or private in-surance regulation, will be discussed only as they affect this main goal. There are two broad classes of economic consequences of insurance coverage for the previously uninsured that have been discussed for decades. One is financial protection; absent insurance coverage, and given the incompleteness of charity care and other aspects of the safety net, uninsured households with moderate incomes could find them-selves liable for relatively large out-of-pocket payments—insurance provides that security. The other goal is access to care: insurance posi-tively affects the use of care, and sometimes that additional use may be of social benefit.

These two consequences of insurance, in my view, become social goals when citizen-taxpayers place positive value on programs that assure greater financial protection and access to care for more of their fellow citizens. Since the great majority of Americans have and will continue to have health insurance, the primary benefit to them from the program arises from extension of coverage to others, al-though there may be some safety net benefits they value for them-selves. In this framework, one can think of a kind of altruistic but real external diseconomy generated by financial distress or medical dis-tress experienced by one's fellow citizens. The positive impact of coverage on use (which would take the form of efficiency reducing moral hazard when middle-class coverage is carried too far) may well be benign in the setting of moving a low-income person from no coverage to at least some coverage. Moreover, there is considerable evidence that increasing insurance coverage in a market area improves the quality of care available to the currently insured (Pagán and Pauly 2006). For all these reasons, then, one might expect taxpayers to attach positive values to a program that reduces the number of uninsured.

With that preference as background, here is how health reform might have been discussed. Take the form of the subsidy program, a set of income-related subsidies to coverage that itself is required to grow in actuarial value as income falls, as given, and imagine that the income-premium subsidy schedule and the income-actuarial value schedule together describe the subsidy program. Subsidies through the exchanges go up to 400 percent of the poverty line, and lower-income households can only use subsidies for generous coverage. For a given definition of broadly eligible populations, providing more generous subsidies as a proportion of premium at any income level (and necessarily extending subsidies further up the income distribution) increases the tax cost of any reform program. In a similar way, holding the proportional subsidy constant but increasing the generosity of coverage also has a positive incremental tax cost.

To translate these higher total spending levels into taxes for individuals we need to specify a tax-sharing rule. For purposes of this discussion let us start by assuming that financing would come through pro-rata increases in the federal income tax. Then a voter would favor an increase in either dimension of generosity as long as his or her valuation of that increase exceeded the incremental tax cost. Given some collective choice rule that maps voters' preferences into collective decisions, the political equilibrium configuration would be the one preferred by the decisive voter, given that voter's valuation of the benefits from extending subsidized coverage to the uninsured relative to that voter's taxes. As long as the tax-sharing rule is not challenged, this should be and remain a political equilibrium.

This idealistic "public choice" model of the political decision process was obviously not what happened during the development and passage of the health reform legislation; general taxpayers were not asked if they were willing to pay higher taxes to see the uninsured covered. Instead, candidate Obama made promises that challenged legislative drafters to come up with a program that would substantially reduce the number of uninsured, with tax increases largely limited to very high income levels and with no imposed changes on coverage or premiums for the insured portion of the population. As a result, the bulk of the cost of subsidies was paid for by reductions in payments for Medicare, especially payments for private Medicare plans, supplemented by (in modest compromise) a tax on high-cost health plans that might by 2018 eventually burden the middle class. Moreover, to keep down the cost of subsidies, the program was designed to achieve target efficiency by directing subsidies only to some lower-income households, those in employment settings (not employed or employed by small firms) where the relative frequency of lack of insurance was greater than among lower-wage households employed in medium-to-large firms.

In the short run, this admirable piece of legislative craftsmanship has caused some resistance among those Medicare beneficiaries who had taken advantage of the often more generous private plans whose government contributions were to be cut, and there was some union protest of the "Cadillac tax" on high-cost health plans. However, neither of these reactions reflects the long-run incidence of the financing that was put in place, nor the political stability of the plan.

Let me deal with the Medicare financing first. It is well known that the Medicare program has substantial financial difficulties as the population ages and costly but beneficial new technology continues to be applied to care for seniors. The real problem is, of course, not the fictitious balance in the Medicare Part A trust fund but, rather, the increased future tax rates borne largely by the working population as growing Medicare spending needs to be financed. The changes in Medicare—reducing Medicare Advantage payment and some other reimbursement reductions to hospitals and doctors (the latter already in great jeopardy)—had been considered possible modifications to Medicare that might have mitigated the worrisome and probably unsustainable tax burden for transfers to the elderly through Medicare and Social Security. Now that these provisions have instead been used to finance transfers to the uninsured, the high burden of future Medicare financing will remain without modification. Who bears this cost depends on what happens next. If the high tax burden induces reductions in social insurance programs for the elderly, they will pay yet further for coverage of the rest of the population. If, despite the dramatically higher tax rates for these programs, they are sustained in something like their current form, middle-class taxpayers and workers in the future will in effect bear the cost of covering the uninsured. They do this not because they were asked to pay higher explicit taxes for health reform but, rather, because they will have to pay higher taxes for Medicare to replace the savings that were transferred to funding health reform.

It is implausible to imagine that taxpayers would fully understand the tortuous process of health reform financing and its incidence. Instead, what is likely to happen is this: the high cost of Medicare, along with the continuation of other aspects of the U.S. federal budgetary problem, means that, when large subsidies for the uninsured are due to begin, taxpayers will be facing high and rising marginal tax rates to pay for Medicare and Social Security. They may then ask to contemplate potential reductions in those taxes from delaying, trimming, or modifying the implementation of the subsidy program for the uninsured. Had they already determined that the current level of subsidies was worth the higher cost they will pay—what was envisioned in my idealistic scenario—the program embodying those subsidies should be politically stable. But if instead they come to realize for the first time how much this generous program is costing them, they may ask for better evidence on the benefits from it and, if the evidence is lacking, cut back on the program in order to hold down their overall federal taxes.

If this day of reckoning comes, what evidence can be offered on the improved health benefits from reducing the number of uninsured? My view is that there is some evidence of positive health effects, and fairly strong evidence at least on benefit (if not on value) for the minority of uninsured who are poor and near poor, but there is woefully weak evidence for the rest of the uninsured. There is also some basis for "selfish" quality benefits to the insured, and perhaps some spillovers from lower financial distress. But the case at present, that subsidies will improve health, is far from compelling and needs to be strengthened if the program is to be politically stable.

In particular, there is good evidence that the absence of insurance does harm to the health of poor people. The evidence comes from changes in Medicaid policy that expanded or contracted eligibility. When fewer people became eligible for Medicaid, the number of poor uninsured rose, and their health suffered. There are many studies lumping all the uninsured together that produce similar results, probably driven by the experience of the poor. But there are few studies that show what happens when non-poor people are uninsured in terms of health outcomes. These non-poor uninsured are generally young people with moderate incomes, which in itself makes it hard to pick up health outcomes. They do report having more frequent times when they did not receive the care they thought was needed because of lack of insurance, but the causal link between failure to get this care and significant harm to health has not been documented. I believe there probably is a link between uninsurance and health for this subpopulation, though one less strong than for the poor, but the mere existence of some negative health effects may not persuade taxpayers to spend more. How large the impact must be so it is persuasive is, of course, unknown, but without evidence on the size of the impact it becomes hard to make the case for justifying several thousands of dollars more in taxes per taxpaying household to pay for health reform.

There is, however, also some good news about financing, but it needs to be reframed properly. A substantial additional amount of funding could be raised by imposing taxes on worker compensation paid in the form of benefits, thus limiting the value of the tax exclusion, and this tax would have the further advantage of encouraging cost-containing insurance policies (Pauly 2009). Note that the tax would cause increased cost sharing and strengthen managed care among the middle class and above who are already insured; results of the RAND health insurance experiment strongly suggest that there will be little adverse impact on health but considerable reduction in spending. Moving up the current high-cost insurance tax to more recent implementation and redefining it as a tax on higher wageworkers who take more generous policies would help both transparency and implementation.

This is a tax with a negative excess burden, one that both raises revenue and corrects already existing distortions, so in that sense it is ideal public policy from the point of view of economic welfare. However, the workers with generous benefits who find their benefits either taxed or curtailed may not see it that way. One way to focus on the benefits is to offset at least part of the capping of the exclusion by lower marginal tax rates; doing this in the context of overall tax reform, as has recently been proposed by recent deficit reduction commissions, might make this step politically feasible, if not exactly attractive.

Finally, the current design of health reform, while offering generous subsidies, does not offer the same subsidies to all workers earning the same income. Instead, subsidies are much greater for lower-income workers in small firms or firms that do not offer insurance coverage (often the same), which is both inequitable to lower-income workers in large firms and likely to cause distortions in firm size as large firms spin off low-wage activities to smaller firms that can qualify for subsidies (Herring and Pauly 2010). Government's ability to keep different sets of low-wage workers apart in order to offer much larger subsidies to some than to others is likely to erode over time. But subsidizing everyone raises the cost of subsidies.

This is a genuine dilemma, and it is the strongest argument about why we might expect some cutbacks in the generosity of subsidies to be seriously discussed. Here better information on benefits from subsidies might help sustain even higher taxes. But it is likely that there will need to be some sort of compromise at a lower level of generosity of benefits and subsidy. The time to start the conversation about what really is the highest priority and highest value is now.

REFERENCES AND FURTHER READING

Herring, B., and M. V. Pauly. 2010. " 'Pay or Play' Insurance Reforms for Employers: Confusion and Inequity." *New England Journal of Medicine* 36, no. 2: 93–95. Available at http://healthpolicyandreform .nejm.org/?p=2626.

Pagán, J. A., and M. V. Pauly. 2006. "Community-Level Uninsurance and Unmet Medical Needs of Insured and Uninsured Adults." *Health Services Research* 41, no. 3: 788–803. Available at www.ncbi .nlm.nih.gov/pmc/articles/ PMC1713201.

Pauly, M. V. 2009. "Limiting the Tax Exclusion for Employment-Based Health Insurance: Are Improved Equity and Efficiency Enough?" *National Tax Journal* 62, no. 3: 555–62. Available at http://findarticles .com/p/articles/mi_hb3356/is_3_62/ai_n42049699.

PART **II**

FINANCIAL MARKET REGULATORY REFORM

CHAPTER 7

Financial Regulatory Reform:
The Politics of Denial

Richard A. Posner

THE PRINCIPAL UNDERLYING causes of the financial crisis that engulfed the nation (and the world) in the fall of 2008 were unsound monetary policy and other regulatory failures. But government officials insist on blaming the private sector and have crafted their proposals for financial regulatory reform accordingly. As a result, those proposals are not well designed to prevent a future such financial debacle.

The Obama administration has proposed an ambitious program of financial regulatory reform, intended to prevent a recurrence of the financial collapse of September (2008). The main elements of the program were sketched in a Treasury Department white paper issued on June 17 of this year; additional details have emerged since, most recently a proposal by the Federal Reserve to regulate the compensation

Richard A. Posner is a judge in the U.S. Court of Appeals for the Seventh Circuit; Senior Lecturer, University of Chicago Law School; and author of *A Failure of Capitalism: The Crisis of '08 and the Descent into Depression* (Cambridge, Mass.: Harvard University Press, 2009).

practices of the banks that it regulates (banks that belong to the Federal Reserve System).

The most important proposals, besides the one just mentioned, are, first, to constitute the Federal Reserve the "systemic risk regulator" of the entire banking system, with "banking" defined to include all or virtually all types of financial intermediaries, including broker-dealers, investment banks, hedge funds, money-market funds, industrial loan companies (such as GE Credit), mortgage banks, and insurance companies, as well as commercial banks and thrifts. The Fed would be empowered to classify any financial company whose failure might endanger the entire financial system as a "Tier 1 Financial Holding Company (FHC)," and to require the company to take measures, such as reducing its leverage, increasing its cash reserves, or altering its compensation practices, designed to reduce the risk of the company's failing (and carrying the rest of the financial sector down with it). The Fed would also be empowered to liquidate or reorganize a failing Tier 1 FHC by means of the kind of informal "resolution" authority that the Federal Deposit Insurance Corporation (FDIC) has been given to wind up the affairs of a failing bank whose deposits the FDIC insures. The most recent proposals would extend the Fed's regulatory power to the compensation practices of all commercial banks—of which there are some eight thousand—rather than just the Tier 1 FHCs.

The second most important proposal is to create a Consumer Financial Regulatory Commission. It would take over the consumer protection functions now exercised by bank regulators and the Federal Trade Commission and would be given comprehensive power to regulate consumer financial products, such as mortgages and credit cards, not only to prevent fraud and deception but also to steer consumers away from risky investments that they may not understand fully. As proposed, the Commission would employ the insights of behavioral economics to identify such investments and nudge consumers away from them. But Congress is unwilling to confer a broad "nudging" power on the Commission, and so that part of the proposal has been abandoned.

SOURCES OF THE CURRENT CRISIS

In focusing on the risks to the financial system that are created by risky banking practices, by compensation schemes that create incentives for traders and loan officers to make risky deals, and by risk-taking by consumers of financial products who succumb to the blandishments of sellers of the products, the administration (and the Fed, which concurs in the administration's recommendations, except that it wants to retain its function of protecting consumers of financial products that are sold by the banks that the Fed regulates) is deflecting attention from the two major causes of the financial debacle of September (2008). The first is profoundly flawed monetary policy, and the second is the ignorance and inattention of the regulatory agencies, notably the Fed itself, the other bank regulatory agencies, and the Securities and Exchange Commission (SEC), which regulates broker-dealers, such as the defunct Lehman Brothers. (The other major broker-dealers before the collapse—Bear Stearns, Merrill Lynch, Goldman Sachs, and Morgan Stanley—have either merged with commercial banks or converted to bank holding companies, in either event coming under the regulatory authority of banking regulators rather than, as before, of the SEC.)

Monetary policy was incompetent, and the regulators of financial intermediaries were asleep at the switch. These are problems that will not be cured even if all the administration's recommendations are adopted.

The likeliest explanation for why these regulatory failures are being ignored is that the government's senior economic officials—Ben Bernanke, Timothy Geithner, and Lawrence Summers—were implicated in the failures and therefore do not want to draw attention to them. We are in the presence of the politics of denial.

Bernanke supported Alan Greenspan's "easy money" policy of the early 2000s, when Bernanke was a member of the Fed's Board of Governors. Later in 2005, as chairman of the President's Council of Economic Advisers, Bernanke denied the existence of a housing bubble just a few months before it began leaking air. Last fall, when the financial collapse occurred, Bernanke and Geithner (then president of the Federal Reserve Bank of New York), along with Henry Paulson, the Secretary of the Treasury, were the nation's principal economic officials. They not only failed to see the collapse coming; they also were responsible for the disastrous decision to allow Lehman Brothers to fail. Bernanke defends the decision on the ground that the Fed lacked legal authority to bail out Lehman because Lehman lacked good enough collateral. The defense is unconvincing. The Federal Reserve Act permits the Fed to make a loan to a nonbank if the loan is "secured to the [Fed's] satisfaction." In the emergency circumstances created by a collapsing global financial system, the Fed could have declared itself "satisfied" with whatever security Lehman could have offered. The idea, which originates with Walter Bagehot (Bagehot 1897), that a central bank should lend as a last resort only upon good collateral is designed for liquidity crises ("panics"), not for insolvency. Until sometime in October, Bernanke and Paulson thought that the seizing up of international finance was a liquidity crisis rather than a solvency crisis.

Geithner defends the failure to save Lehman on the equally unconvincing ground that such a bailout might have cost the government a trillion dollars. The most plausible explanation for the failure is that Bernanke, Geithner, and Paulson did not anticipate the consequences of the failure, in part because (I am surmising) they did not understand the critical role that Lehman played in the commercial paper, letter of credit, and credit-default swap markets, and in part because they did not foresee that the failure to save Lehman would cause a run by hedge funds on the other broker-dealers, imperiling them, which in turn caused a run on the hedge funds by *their* investors.

Summers and Geithner, along with Robert Rubin (Rubin and Summers being in succession Secretaries of the Treasury in the Clinton administration), were complacent about the growing risk-taking of banks and other financial intermediaries and opposed the regulation of credit-default swaps, now recognized to have contributed to the financial collapse. Even though housing prices began their long, steep decline early in 2006 and the banking industry (especially the "shadow banking" industry of broker-dealers and other "nonbank banks") was known to be very heavily invested in mortgage lending, the Federal Reserve, the SEC, and other regulators of financial practices and products did little to avert financial disaster because they underestimated the looming losses to banks' loan portfolios as housing prices fell and defaults rose. Until Lehman Brothers collapsed, the regulators didn't realize how serious the situation was, even though the financial collapse had been building since the middle of 2007 and accelerating since March 2008, when Bear Stearns collapsed.

The major underlying cause of the financial crisis was the decision by Greenspan (supported by Bernanke when he became a member of the Fed's Board of Governors in 2002) to force short-term interest rates way down. Fearing deflation in the wake of the recession triggered by the collapse of the dot-com bubble in 2000, Greenspan engineered a drastic reduction in the federal funds rate, which influences short-term interest rates (including interest rates on adjustable-rate mortgages, which Greenspan encouraged) directly, and long-term interest rates, such as mortgage rates, indirectly, into negative territory (in real, that is, inflation-adjusted terms). Such rates, in an economy with minimal unemployment, were bound to be inflationary (low interest rates increase the amount of money in circulation). But because of rapidly growing productivity and cheap foreign imports, particularly from China, inflationary pressure was deflected from the goods and services that dominate the consumer price index to assets, particularly houses and common stock. The result was an asset-price inflation that turned into a housing bubble and a stock bubble.

Such linked bubbles are known from Japanese experience in the 1990s to pose serious dangers to a nation's financial system. To these dangers the Fed remained indifferent until it was too late.

So one would like to see proposals for improving the Federal Reserve's management of monetary policy (such as taking seriously John Taylor's "Taylor Rule" for determining the optimal federal funds rate) and, what is closely related, improving the Fed's financial intelligence in both senses of the word "intelligence"—information about events, trends, institutions, and practices relating to financial intermediation and competent analysis of developments in that field. Of course, politically, as well as from the standpoint of the *amour propre* of key officials such as Bernanke, the populist account of the economic crisis, which focuses on the greed and duplicity of "Wall Street" and the plight of the psychologically manipulated consumers of subprime mortgages, is more attractive than focusing on mistakes of regulation by the Federal Reserve and the other financial regulators. This is especially so because the administration wants *more* regulation, not just more vigorous regulation or the rolling back of some of the financial deregulatory measures of recent decades.

The Treasury report acknowledges regulatory mistakes in a vague, general way but instead emphasizes imagined gaps in the overall financial regulatory structure in order to bolster the argument for changes in that structure. Proposals for structural change—new agencies, new authorities, and so forth—are standard government responses to governmental failures. They are more dramatic, and more attention-getting, than suggestions for improving regulatory performance, and usually cheaper; and they buy time—the time it takes to implement the reorganization.

The regulatory agencies have most of the powers they need to minimize the risks of another financial collapse, because the Fed and the SEC have between them plenary regulatory power over almost all major financial intermediaries. And, to expand the Fed's powers at the expense of the SEC's, as the Treasury report proposes, rather than reforming the SEC, will jeopardize the Fed's political independence.

SHOULD OFFICIALS COMPLICIT IN THE CAUSES OF THE CRISIS WRITE THE REFORMS?

Our reform-minded officials need a better understanding of the causes of the 2008 financial collapse, and for that they need to look inward. It is a bad sign that Bernanke and the others refuse to acknowledge their own contribution to the collapse. It is another bad sign that proposals for ambitious regulatory reform have been made, and are being pressed, before the financial crisis has run its course and before there has been an impartial, in-depth study of the causes of the crisis. I have given my own view of those causes in this chapter and at greater length in my book (Posner 2009), but I do not claim that it is definitive. Congress has appointed a Financial Crisis Inquiry Commission (FCIC) to conduct an eighteen-month study of those causes, and reform proposals should be tabled until the study is completed and evaluated—that, or a better study. For I have no great hopes for the FCIC. It is bipartisan rather than nonpartisan, none of its members is a professional economist, and its executive director is a prosecutor. It is likely to embrace the populist theory of the crisis without adequate reflection.

Fortunately there is no great urgency about restructuring the financial regulatory system. Everyone in the system, public and private, is hyperalert to signs of new bubbles and excessive risk-taking. Everyone on the private side is concerned to avoid the kind of risk-triggered failure that invites a government takeover and a congressional inquisition, and everyone on the public side is concerned with steering the economic recovery between the Scylla of economic stagnation (even deflation) and the Charybdis of runaway inflation.

Let us see how the recovery proceeds. There will be time enough to address issues of financial regulatory reform when a restored economy enables such issues to be addressed candidly, not defensively; professionally, not angrily; patiently, not hastily—and by a fresh team, unembarrassed and unconstrained by past errors.

REFERENCES AND FURTHER READING

Bagehot, Walter. 1897. *Lombard Street: A Description of the Money Market*. New York: Charles Scribner's Sons. Available at http://books.google.com/books?id=xl8-AAAAIAAJ&printsec=frontcover&dq=inauthor:Walter+inauthor:Bagehot&l r=&as_dr rb_is=q&as_minm_is=0&as_miny_is=&as_maxm_is=0&as_maxy_is=&as_brr=0#v=onepage&q=&f=false.

Posner, Richard. 2009. *A Failure of Capitalism: The Crisis of '08 and the Descent into Depression*. Cambridge, Mass.: Harvard University Press.

CHAPTER 8

Government Guarantees: Why the Genie Needs to Be Put Back in the Bottle

Viral V. Acharya and Matthew Richardson

WITH GOVERNMENTS BEGINNING to implement new financial regulation, the G20, in its recent Pittsburgh summit, laid out the following four principles on which it will coordinate:

1. building high-quality capital and mitigating pro-cyclicality;
2. improving over-the-counter derivatives markets;
3. arranging better plans for the resolution of cross-border and systemically important financial institutions by the end of 2010; and
4. reforming compensation practices to support financial stability.

Viral V. Acharya and Matthew Richardson are Professors of Finance at the New York University Stern School of Business and coauthors of the book (along with Stijn van Nieuwerburgh and Lawrence White) *Guaranteed to Fail: Fannie Mae, Freddie Mac and the Debacle of Mortgage Finance* (Princeton, N.J.: Princeton University Press, 2011).

Will the proposed reforms do the job? Overhauling the financial system is a tricky thing—but we have been here before.

The last major financial crisis led to the sweeping reforms undertaken in 1934. The Glass Steagall Act insured deposits (up to a threshold amount) to prevent bank runs. In order to address the moral hazard induced by deposit insurance, the Act also restricted commercial banks from undertaking risky security activities. The Federal Deposit Insurance fund was set up to charge premiums against the insurance and to be in charge of resolving failed banks.

WHAT WENT WRONG

While these reforms worked well for over half a century, they became antiquated in the face of modern and global banking. Financial developments allowed U.S. banks to innovate around its restrictions. European banks were all universal, unlike their U.S. counterparts, and did both commercial and investment banking. Competitive forces led to a steady repeal of the Glass Steagall Act. And the liability structure of banks evolved from just deposits, bonds, and equity, to also include recourse from complex off-balance sheet entities and derivatives positions.

In the process, however, banks and other financial institutions grew large, effectively attained too-big-to-fail status, and competed so fiercely with each other that regulatory arbitrage became their primary business model rather than an aside. A shadow banking world of conduits and money market funds grew to several trillion dollars, performing a large chunk of intermediation activity. Traditional banks morphed first into underwriting houses and eventually into casinos: interest margins thinned and fee and trading components of bank revenues ballooned.

Any semblance of doubt that the unregulated shadow banking world was subject to market discipline was erased in this crisis. We bailed out banks brought down by recourse from off-balance sheet vehicles, guaranteed money-market funds, and effectively backstopped over-the-counter guarantees that enabled banks to scale their risks multifold in a few years.

There is little doubt that a part of the problem was that Wall Street had a huge incentive to make carry trades and spread bets, generating false profits and booking the proceeds as profits. But the G20 notion that the failure of governance was (only) between rogue traders and shareholders is false and dangerous.

The fact that bank shareholders ex post took a bath in this crisis doesn't change the fact that they did exceedingly well in the preceding years. All evidence points to shareholders, through their boards, encouraging the risk-taking activities until the game ended. And creditors of large financials did not worry about these risks either. In effect, all risks were being transferred onto the taxpayers.

Though regulators are right that it is tough to fight such moral hazard in the midst of a crisis, one cannot escape the reality that the Wall Street profits were privatized but that its risks have been socialized.

THE NEED TO ADDRESS GOVERNMENTAL FAILURES AS WELL AS MARKET FAILURES

Hence, unlike in 1934, we have a slightly more difficult job on hand. We need to address not just market failures but also regulatory failures arising due to government guarantees.

Mispriced government guarantees are pervasive throughout the financial system—inadequately priced deposit insurance, the too-big-to-fail designation, the too-many-to-fail problem, and subsidies provided to government-sponsored enterprises. These distort risk-taking incentives in the system, and their destabilizing effects percolate to the shadow banking world too.

There is perhaps no greater example of this activity than the cases of Fannie Mae and Freddie Mac. For every dollar that shareholders put up, they borrowed another twenty-five dollars to invest in risky, relatively illiquid pools of subprime mortgages at very attractive spreads. It is no surprise that they ended up accumulating a $1.5 trillion portfolio.

Why did they take such a risky bet? Because they could. Capital markets offered them cheap leverage. Of course, the reason leverage was cheap was that creditors could not care less about risk in the case of Fannie and Freddie—the government had provided an implicit guarantee of the debt.

WHAT TO DO ABOUT GOVERNMENT GUARANTEES?

Correcting this regulatory failure is apparently simple. If we require that financial institutions fully pay in good times for the guarantees they receive ex post, in all likelihood this will organically cause financial firms to no longer take unsound risks.

But charging for government guarantees is not easy. What guarantees are being used for can change quickly. Thus it is worthwhile to assess carefully the available options.

First and foremost, some abuse of government guarantees must be checked at source. In the case of Fannie and Freddie, a complete ring-fencing of guarantees—by shutting down their financial investments arm—is called for. Similarly, if the shadow banking world of conduits has effective recourse to bank balance sheets, it should simply be on bank balance sheets.

However, eliminating all guarantees—especially deposit insurance—is unlikely to be credible or have any political support. And given that some are calling for extending guarantees to money-market deposits and possibly even secured inter-bank borrowing ("repos"), it is important to approach the charge for such guarantees in a principled manner.

It is simply unacceptable that when the FDIC's deposit insurance fund reserves exceed a certain level many banks are no longer required to pay fees into the fund. In fact, large banks did not pay any significant deposit insurance premium for the decade leading up to the crisis, and the insurance funds are now depleted. By not charging for insurance during the run-up to the crisis, the government exacerbated the moral hazard problem.

SYSTEMIC RISK MUST DRIVE THE PREMIUM FOR GOVERNMENT GUARANTEES

Another key insight is that government guarantees do not kick in each time a bank fails. If an individual bank fails, it can be readily sold to others. Even insured deposits are often assumed by acquiring banks. The real problem arises when there is a systemic crisis, that is, when banks fail but no potential acquirers are healthy enough to purchase them. Now the government has to step in and help find a suitor, pay off insured depositors, and often guarantee even the uninsured creditors.

Hence, charging for government guarantees requires charging for an institution's systemic risk rather than its individual risk.

Indeed, there was tremendous, mostly unrecognized, growth in the systemic risk of financial institutions during the period 2004–2007. The best example of this was Wall Street ignoring its own business model of securitization by holding onto the non-diversifiable credit risk associated with the AAA-tranches loan portfolios, particularly tied to residential real estate but also commercial real estate and other consumer credit. This turned out to be a $2–3 trillion one-way asymmetric bet on the economy.

Systemic risk imposes a negative externality on the system because the external cost of a financial institution's collapse—which leads to failures of others and/or the freezing of capital markets—is not internalized by that institution. Since regulations such as Basel capital requirement and deposit insurance premiums focused mostly on individual risk as opposed to system-wide risk, financial firms loaded up on assets with low volatility but high systematic risk and, therefore, higher expected returns than their underpriced cost of borrowing.

Any Econ 101 textbook explains how to resolve negative externalities. Once we recognize that systemic financial institutions are no different than a typical industrial company that pollutes the air with carbon emissions, it becomes clear that the solution is to "tax" the institutions by taking into account their contributions to systemic risk. For instance, the actuarially fair deposit insurance premium— the premium that exactly covers the expected cost to the deposit insurance provider—should not only increase in relation to individual bank failure risk but also in relation to joint bank failure risk.

Of course, the devil is in the details. If regulators simply produce coarse categories of systemic risk of institutions based on size and function, substantial arbitrage will occur at the edges. A group of smaller players (for example, investment banks) can concentrate systemic linkages and be a greater source of risk. Hence, a systemic risk tax must vary smoothly across the dimensions of risk and size.

One possibility is to require each institution to purchase insurance against its losses in predefined crash events. To reduce the moral hazard, the payoffs on the insurance would not go back to the institution but to a systemic risk fund to help with the resolution of the financial sector in a crisis. Equally important, the insurance premium would be paid on a continual basis by the financial institution so that any reduction in the firm's "systemic" risk-taking activities would lower its fees. The insurance could be partly provided by private players to create an actively priced market for systemic insurance of financial institutions. The rest can be provided by the regulators to avoid an American International Group (AIG)-type problem. There is a precedent to such a public-private approach to insuring systemic events, namely, the Terrorism Risk Insurance Act of 2002.

Another possibility is to tie capital requirements to market-based measures of systemic risk. For instance, consider a simple statistical tool—"Marginal Expected Shortfall" (MES)—that measures the average loss of an institution's capitalization when the market is in its, say, 5 percent worst days. MES, which is computed based on data prior to the crisis, does a remarkably good job in predicting those who performed worst during the crisis. For example, the top 10 financial institutions in terms of MES in June 2007 were Citigroup, JP Morgan Chase, Bank of America, Morgan Stanley, Goldman Sachs, Merrill Lynch, Wells Fargo, Fannie Mae, AIG, and Wachovia, by and large a who's who of troubled firms. And though Bear Stearns and Lehman come in 21st and 12th, respectively, these firms are 3rd and 6th, respectively, on a market cap-adjusted basis. It isn't rocket science to figure out who we need to focus on.

RESTORE INCENTIVES AND LET THE MARKET DO THE REST

Some argue that once financial institutions have to fully pay for their guarantees and their systemic risk contribution, it will be so onerous that they will no longer be profitable. However, if banks in their current large and complex form cannot make it without full government backing, then this says more about the business model of large, complex banks than anything else. If we really think the only source of capital is the government, we will have implicitly socialized our private financial system.

Under our proposal, the creative destructive nature of capitalism will solve this problem. Once firms in their current form no longer have access to government freebies, market discipline will come back to the whole financial sector. All financial institutions will have to change their behavior, most likely leading them to spin-off subsidiaries, and become less systemic. This way, the reform of systemic risk will end up being mostly organic and incentive-based rather than requiring the heavy hand of government.

It is a little disconcerting, however, that throughout this crisis regulators have gone in the opposite direction. Mergers have been encouraged that create more systemically important institutions, for example, Bank of America–Merrill Lynch–Countrywide, JP Morgan Chase–Bear Stearns, JP Morgan Chase–Washington Mutual, Wells Fargo–Wachovia, and so forth. As incredible as it might seem, the scarcity of strong balance sheets in the financial sector means that institutions with full government guarantees, such as Fannie Mae and Freddie Mac, now wield even more power than before the crisis. In recent months the money-market sector, the asset-backed securities loan market, and the debt of financial firms were effectively given the full backing of the U.S. government, greatly expanding issues related to moral hazard.

While some of this may have been necessary, now we will have to find some way to put the genie back in the bottle. The aforementioned proposals should help do the trick.

REFERENCES AND FURTHER READING

Acharya, V., T. Cooley, M. Richardson, and I. Walter, eds. 2010. *Regulating Wall Street: The Dodd-Frank Act and the New Architecture of Global Finance*. Hoboken, N.J.: John Wiley & Sons.

Acharya, V., S. Nieuwerburgh, M. Richardson, and L. White. 2011. *Guaranteed to Fail: Fannie Mae, Freddie Mac and the Debacle of Mortgage Finance*. Princeton, N.J.: Princeton University Press.

Acharya, V., L. Pedersen, T. Philippon, and M. Richardson. 2009. "Measuring Systemic Risk." Working Paper, Stern School, New York University Stern School of Business.

Acharya, V., and M. Richardson, eds. 2009. *Restoring Financial Stability: How to Repair a Failed System*. Hoboken, N.J.: John Wiley & Sons.

CHAPTER 9

How Little We Know:
The Challenges of Financial Reform

Russell Roberts

WHEN AN AIRPLANE crashes, expert investigators probe the cause of the crash. Their analysis can lead to changes in aircraft design, flight procedures, and regulations in hopes of reducing the likelihood of a future crash. The growth of knowledge in the airline industry has been extremely productive. Between 1989 and 2008, there was a sevenfold reduction in the probability of a fatal crash.

There is a natural tendency for economists (and even for normal people) to presume that similar analytical techniques can be applied to financial crashes. After all, economists presumably know more than we did in the past. We have ever more data and ever more sophisticated techniques for analyzing the data. Yet there is no evidence to suggest that financial market regulation is more effective than in the past. If anything, the opposite appears to be the case.

Russell Roberts is Professor of Economics at George Mason University, a Mercatus Center scholar, and a Research Scholar at Stanford University's Hoover Institution. He blogs at Cafe Hayek and hosts the weekly podcast EconTalk.

This discouraging empirical record does not seem to hamper the unending stream of ideas for what might make our financial system more secure, based on an analysis of what went wrong this time. It is obvious, for example, that excessive leverage played a role in the vulnerability of the firms that collapsed in 2008. The natural response is to increase capital requirements.

The incentives of management on Wall Street appear to be out of line with the interests of both investors and taxpayers, leading to suggestions for caps on executive compensation or changes in the mix between cash and other forms of compensation. As an example, the Obama administration pay czar, Kenneth Feinberg, has limited take-home pay for executives at firms receiving government assistance and offset the reduction with increases in stock that would not be accessible for two to four years. The hope is to encourage the growth of long-term investing instead of riskier, short-term bets.

Despite the spectacular failure of Fannie Mae and Freddie Mac, some economists insist that Fannie and Freddie need to be kept in place but, somehow, just made safer. This optimistic advocacy—which assumes that Fannie and Freddie are like airplanes that need better landing gear—is in spite of the fact that between 1992 and 2008 Fannie and Freddie had their own regulator—the Office of Federal Housing Enterprises Oversight—that failed to stop the meltdown of Fannie and Freddie and has cost the U.S. taxpayer about $150 billion and counting. Somehow, this time will be different.

EMERGENT ORDER, FEEDBACK LOOPS, AND UNINTENDED CONSEQUENCES

I am not so optimistic about reforming the government-sponsored enterprises or the system of regulation and supervision of Wall Street. Our financial system is unlike an airplane. It is complex in a way that makes even an airplane look simple. A synthetic collateralized debt obligation has something of the complexity of an airplane. The financial system is much more complex. It is an emergent system, where outcomes are the result of a dynamic interaction between investors, regulators, and politicians.

Economists have a very imperfect understanding of this interaction. Because of the feedback loops between the different actors in the system, we also have a very imperfect understanding of how changing one piece of the system interacts with the rest of the system. Landing gear that is more reliable makes an airplane safer, but reducing risk or changing incentives in one part of the financial system can cause less transparent changes elsewhere that reduce stability. Recognizing the meagerness of our understanding would be a good starting place for what should be a humble approach to financial reform.

For example, advocating "better" supervision or "more vigorous" regulation or even something more specific such as larger capital cushions ignores the empirical record that regulators and politicians, either for venal or human reasons, seem unable to maintain these restrictions in the face of pressure from participants. Even detailed, specific plans are unlikely to succeed because of feedback loops that are present in all emergent systems.

As F. A. Hayek said in *The Fatal Conceit*: "The curious task of economics is to demonstrate to men how little they really know about what they imagine they can design." There are few better illustrations of this than the attempts to engineer a financial system that preserves the incentives to take risks and at the same time preserves prudence. We imagine we can design a better financial system. Perhaps it is time to concede that such a top-down enterprise is inherently flawed.

Economists who treat the financial system like an airplane ignore the symbiotic dance between politicians, on the one hand, and financial institutions, on the other.

The revolving doors between Fannie Mae and government, and between Goldman Sachs and government, are only the most obvious indicators that something is wrong. A Martian impartially observing the U.S. financial system would conclude that it is run to benefit the executives and protégés of Goldman Sachs. This is not a good thing, even if it is not true. If it is true, then any meaningful financial reform must start with finding ways to break that symbiosis.

Most reforms ignore that symbiosis, condemn capitalism as inherently unstable, and look for ways to artificially create the right incentives. But the government, because of that symbiosis and other political incentives, played a significant role in reducing the stability of the system and perverting the incentives that would naturally emerge. In particular, policy makers have been too eager to cushion creditors from the consequences of financing imprudent risk-taking using large amounts of borrowed money.

THE CONSEQUENCES OF RESCUING CREDITORS
OF LARGE FINANCIAL INSTITUTIONS

The rescues of the last twenty-five years, starting with Continental Illinois in 1984, up through the Fed-orchestrated intervention to prevent the collapse of Long Term Capital Management in 1998, the rescue of Mexico and its creditors in 1995, and the implicit guarantee of Fannie and Freddie, reduced the incentive of counterparties, particularly lenders, to restrain the highly leveraged bets that ended up wreaking so much financial havoc.

It's obvious why financial institutions prefer borrowing other people's money rather than using their own. But why didn't debt issuers restrain risk-taking as Wall Street firms pursued riskier investments? Part of the reason is that they anticipated the possibility of government rescue, particularly as their lending made them increasingly entangled with each other.

The importance of moral hazard, described presciently in 2004 by Gary Stern and Ron Feldman (see Stern and Feldman 2004), is often greeted with skepticism because of what seems to be the restraints on recklessness imposed by equity holders. After all, the skeptics point out, Jimmy Cayne, the CEO of Bear Stearns, and Richard Fuld, the CEO of Lehman Brothers, each lost $1 billion (yes, with a "b") from the collapse of the value of their companies' stocks from earlier highs. Surely this limits the moral hazard problem.

But Cayne and Fuld could not access those paper profits at will. More importantly, each man is worth in the neighborhood of $500 million, wealth they accumulated through cash compensation and the occasional judicious sale of their companies' stock in advance of the crash. Yes, there was a lot of myopia and overconfidence on Wall Street. But when people spend their own money, they spend it more carefully. Cayne and Fuld doubled down with other people's money. They were more prudent with their own.

Reasonable people can debate the magnitude of the responsibility that past rescues played in the excessive risk-taking that destroyed much of Wall Street. But the subsequent rescue of Bear Stearns, Merrill, Citigroup, Fannie and Freddie, and AIG has certainly set significant expectations for the future. (For further discussions of the role of past creditor rescue in encouraging reckless risk-taking, see Roberts 2010.)

The solution seems simple. Rather than try to turn this dial or push that lever connected to some part of the system just the right amount (holding everything else constant, somehow), we should let natural feedback loops emerge that encourage prudence as well as risk-taking. For these natural feedback loops to emerge, we must get rid of the doctrine of "too big to fail" or maybe "too connected to fail" or at least "too connected to Goldman Sachs to fail."

But even otherwise optimistic economists understand that this prescription is unlikely to succeed given the incentives of politicians and policy makers to avoid short-run damage in favor of meltdowns that come to pass in the long run, where they may not be dead but are at least out of office. Yet without rescinding the implicit policy of bailing out the creditors of large financial institutions, there will be

inadequate incentives to restrain excessive leverage and the impru-
dence that inevitably follows when people are allowed to gamble with
other people's money. Attempts to repair the system from the top
down will fail. We must find ways to let bottom-up solutions emerge.

WHAT CAN BE DONE?

These observations suggest a very modest program for reform:

Don't try to re-create the old system while trying to make it "better." There is a natural wariness about securitization right now. That
is good. Let it blossom. There is a natural wariness about zero-down
mortgages. That is good. Let it blossom.

Recognize that having every American own a home is not the
American Dream but the dream of the National Association of Home
Builders and the National Association of Realtors. Any government
programs to increase home ownership should be funded out of current tax dollars where the costs are visible. Get rid of mandates such as
the Community Reinvestment Act. Get rid of Fannie and Freddie and
the implicit guarantee that turned out to be only too real.

Be aware that the Fed is certainly part of the problem and may not
be part of the solution. The Fed created the artificially low interest
rates that helped inflate the housing bubble. The Fed then raised interest rates too quickly with disastrous effects for the adjustable-rate
mortgages encouraged by their low-interest rate policy. Monetary
policy should not be left to any self-proclaimed or publicly anointed
maestro. Following an automatic money growth rule or the Taylor
rule would have avoided much of the pain. Somebody needs to hold
the Fed accountable for funding exuberance.

In addition, the Fed has played a major role in exacerbating the
moral hazard problem. It needs to be restrained rather than empowered. It is not good for a democracy to have an agency as unaccount-
able as the Fed acquire even more power and use it in ad hoc ways.

Capitalism is a profit and loss system. The profits encourage risk-taking. The losses encourage prudence. These natural feedback loops have been distorted by the rescues of the past and the present. We need to take the "crony" out of crony capitalism. That will not be easy. But economists should not make it more difficult. The near-universal praise by economists for the actions of Bernanke, Paulson, and Geithner, and the near-universal condemnation by economists of the decision to let Lehman Brothers enter bankruptcy, greatly reduces the credibility of any promise by policy makers to act differently in the future.

Over the last fifteen months, average Americans have sent hundreds of billions of dollars to some of the richest people in human history. The better the citizenry understands this reality, the better chance the political incentives will change. If people don't understand it, the political incentives are going to stay in place. Economists play an important role in how people perceive what has happened. We should stop being the enablers of such obscene transfers of wealth.

Policy makers who make creditors and lenders whole should be excoriated, condemned, and called to account rather than praised and honored. Zero cents on the dollar for bankrupt bets made by lenders and creditors would be ideal but is unlikely to be a credible promise. So let's start more modestly. A ceiling of fifty cents on the dollar for creditors and lenders when the institutions they fund become insolvent is a natural place to start. Even this may be too difficult for politicians to stomach. But economists should at least preach the virtues of letting creditors lose money when they finance imprudent risk-takers.

We are what we repeatedly do—not what we say we are or not what we'd like to be but what we do. What we do as a body politic is rescue rich people from the consequences of their decisions. That is bad for democracy and bad for capitalism. Until we fix that, we as citizens are playing a game of "heads—Wall Street executives win a ridiculously enormous amount, tails—they just win a ridiculous amount, paid for by the rest of us." Until we fix that, little else matters.

REFERENCES AND FURTHER READING

Hayek, F. A. 1991. *The Fatal Conceit: The Errors of Socialism.* Chicago: University of Chicago Press.

Lucchetti, A., David Enrich, and Joann Lublin. 2009. "Fed Hits Banks with Sweeping Pay Limits." *Wall Street Journal*, October 23. Available at http://online.wsj.com/article/SB125623026446601619.html.

Roberts, Russell. 2010. "Gambling with Other People's Money: How Policy Mistakes Created Perverse Incentives and the Financial Crisis of 2008." Mercatus Center, George Mason University. Available at http://mercatus.org/publication/gambling-other-peoples-money.

Solomon, Deborah. 2009. "Pay Czar Targets Salary Cuts." *Wall Street Journal*, October 6. Available at http://online.wsj.com/article/SB12547 8783753066235.html.

Stern, Gary, and Ron Feldman. 2004. *Too Big to Fail: The Hazards of Bank Bailouts.* Washington, D.C.: Brookings Institution Press. (Reissued in 2009.)

Thompson, Andrea. 2009. "Flying Is Safer than Ever." LiveScience (June 1). Available at www.livescience.com/culture/090601-air-crashes .html.

CHAPTER 10

Finding the Sweet Spot for Effective Regulation

R. Glenn Hubbard

THE CONVENTIONAL TAKE on the present financial and economic crisis places blame on a dearth of regulation. But that is simplistic at best, entirely inaccurate at worst. The truth is that the financial crisis is the result of not so much a lack of regulation as a lack of *effective* regulation.

Indeed, portions of the financial system hit hard by the crisis and significantly affecting economic activity—such as traditional banks—have historically been the most heavily regulated. Another center of the crisis was government-sponsored entities such as Fannie Mae and Freddie Mac, which were vehicles through which governmental capital made its impact on the financial markets. While more regulation is certainly needed in some areas, as I describe later, the overriding goal must be to make the present regulatory regime far more effective than it has been.

R. Glenn Hubbard, a former Chairman of the Council of Economic Advisers under President George W. Bush, is Dean of Columbia Business School and Co-Chair of the Committee on Capital Markets Regulation.

A focus on effectiveness leads to three themes for reform. The primary one should be the reduction of systemic risk. The second is that the route to enhanced investor protection is through greater transparency in the financial system. The third is that the U.S. regulatory structure must be reorganized to meet these two goals—that is, it must become more integrated and efficient. These themes are highlighted in the report released in 2009 by the nonpartisan Committee on Capital Markets Regulation,[1] which I co-chair.

MORE EFFECTIVE REGULATION AND SYSTEMIC RISK

When a systemically important institution is in danger of failure, and its failure could trigger a chain reaction of other failures, there may be no alternative other than to inject public funds. But the requisite amount of these injections has been significantly increased by weaknesses in the current regulatory system. The Federal Reserve financed the acquisition of Bear Stearns through a $29 billion loan, and the Fed and the Treasury financed the survival of the American International Group with assistance amounting to more than $180 billion, largely because of the fear of what would have happened if such institutions had gone into bankruptcy. Similar fears may lie behind some of the Troubled Asset Relief Program injections. There is ample room for improvement in the containment of systemic risk.

First, existing capital requirements leave much to be desired. The elaborate and detailed structure currently in place to regulate bank capital, the international Basel Accord, proved unable to live up to the task of preventing systemically important financial institutions from failing. Indeed, the crude leverage ratio—an object of scorn of many regulators—turned out to be a more reliable constraint on excessive risk-taking than the complex Basel rules. The investment banking sector, which did not have a leverage ratio in its regulation, was not as fortunate. The disparity demonstrates that more detailed regulation does not necessarily make for more effective regulation. Capital requirements are our principal bulwark against bank failure, a key trigger of systemic risk, but can be improved. Larger banks should have higher capital ratios, and the leverage ratio should be reduced. This approach is a much better one than putting size limits on U.S. banks, which will make them uncompetitive with their European and Asian counterparts.

Three changes to capital requirement recommendations would be a foundation for improved stability. As a consequence of the crisis, many systemically important institutions will be able to borrow from the Federal Reserve. And institutions that have the ability to borrow from the Fed in its lender-of-last-resort role should be subject to capital regulation. In addition, given the cyclicality of bank losses, a fixed capital requirement forces banks to raise capital in a downturn as losses mount and capital levels are depleted. An alternative to letting capital requirements fall during a downturn would be to allow, or require, banks to hold some form of contingent capital (through publicly or privately provided insurance) as losses mount. Finally, given the concentration of risks to taxpayers, large institutions should be held to a higher solvency standard—that is, they should hold more capital per unit of risk. The market can also play a role in this process: if investors are given more information about the solvency of banks, as was given to them by the stress tests, they can demand more capital from banks.

Second, we need a better process than bankruptcy for resolving the insolvency of financial institutions. Our framework for banks needs to be extended to other financial institutions and their holding companies. This process, unlike bankruptcy, puts the resolution of institutions in the hands of regulators rather than bankruptcy judges and permits more flexible approaches to keeping systemically important institutions afloat. At the same time, it permits, like bankruptcy, the restructuring of an insolvent institution through the elimination of equity and the restructuring of debt, to prepare the institution for sale to new investors. We do not need to create a special regime for systemically important bank holding companies, as the Dodd-Frank Act does, but we need to extend the features of the current Federal Deposit Insurance Corporation regime from just banks to all financial institutions.

Third, the current substantive framework also suffers from important gaps in the scope and coverage of regulation—gaps that can increase the risk of shocks to the financial system. Hedge funds and private equity firms have not been supervised or regulated. Fannie Mae and Freddie Mac were too lightly regulated; until the Housing and Economic Recovery Act of 2008, they were not subject to either meaningful capital or securities regulation. Investment bank regulation by the Securities and Exchange Commission proved entirely ineffective—major investment banks have failed, been acquired, or become bank holding companies. We need a comprehensive approach to regulating risk in the financial sector if we are to avoid similar threats to the financial system in the future. Casting a broader net does not mean that different activities should be regulated in the same way, but it does mean that the same activities conducted by different institutions should be regulated in the same way.

Hedge funds (and banks that engage in hedge fund activity) should keep regulators informed on an ongoing basis of their activities and leverage. Private equity, however, poses no more risk to the financial system than do other investors. But these firms, if large enough, should be subject to some regulatory oversight and periodically share information with regulators to confirm they are engaged only in the private equity business. Indeed, private equity is a part of the solution to the problem of inadequate private capital in the banking system. Ill-conceived restrictions on the ability of private equity firms to acquire banks should be removed, not just relaxed. This instance is one in which regulation is preventing a solution, not offering one.

Finally, we need to reduce the interconnectedness problem of credit-default swap (CDS) by the use of clearinghouses and exchanges, as in the Dodd-Frank Act. If clearinghouses were to clear CDS contracts and other standardized derivatives, such as foreign exchange and interest rate swaps, systemic risk could be substantially reduced by more netting, centralized information on the exposures of counterparties, and the collectivization of losses. To the extent that certain CDSs were to be traded on exchanges, price discovery and liquidity would be enhanced. I would go further than just encouraging exchange trading; I would require it for standardized and heavily traded derivatives. Increased liquidity would not only be valuable to traders, but it would better enable clearinghouses to control their own risks through more informed margining and easier closeouts of defaulted positions.

GREATER TRANSPARENCY TO PROTECT INVESTORS

Securitization has brought new sources of finance to the consumer market, not only for mortgages but also for auto loans and credit card purchases. It has permitted banks to diversify their risks. Imagine how much more devastating the impact of the fall in home prices would have been on the banking system if all mortgages had been held by banks rather than being mostly securitized (even taking into account the exposure some banks had from investments in the securitized debt itself). There is a great need to rebuild this market from the ground up now that the financial crisis has exposed critical flaws in its operation.

Originators, whether banks or brokers, need stronger incentives to originate loans that are in conformity with what they have promised. Mandatory minimum retention of risk in respect of securitized assets must address a number of important issues in order to be practical and beneficial. Among other things, for example, a minimum risk retention requirement would increase the risk of the banking sector and be difficult to enforce given the possibility of hedging. Furthermore, such a requirement would compel the originator to bear general economic risk—such as risk from interest rate changes—not just the risk of non-conforming assets. A superior solution is to strengthen representations, warranties, and repurchase obligations and require increased disclosure of originators' interests in securitized offerings. Certain high-risk practices, such as "no doc" loans, should be prohibited outright. Moreover, we would increase loan-level disclosures and encourage regulators to study ways of improving the standardized public disclosure package.

Credit rating agencies should be reformed to reinvigorate the securitized debt markets. In order to restore confidence in the integrity of credit ratings and improve how the global fixed-income markets function in the future, I propose developing globally consistent standards, avoiding governmental interference in the rating determination process, reviewing references to credit ratings in regulatory frameworks, and increasing disclosure pertaining to ratings of structured finance and other securities.

MORE EFFECTIVE REGULATORY STRUCTURE

Even after the passage of the Dodd-Frank Act, the U.S. financial regulatory framework is highly fragmented and ineffective. The fragmentation of regulators is not the product of careful design—it has evolved by layers of accretion since the Civil War. It has survived largely unchanged, despite repeated unsuccessful efforts at reform. The current crisis has demonstrated that this dysfunctional system comes with a very high cost. In contrast to the route taken in the Dodd-Frank Act, a statement by the Committee on Capital Markets Regulation, entitled "Recommendations for Reorganizing the U.S. Regulatory Structure,"[2] proposed a new consolidated structure, comprising the Fed, a newly created U.S. Financial Services Authority, the Treasury Department, and possibly a consumer and investor protection agency. This structure can substantially reduce the risk of future financial crises. I disagree with calls for a systemic risk council. The Dodd-Frank solution is only more fragmentation by another name.

Any existing Fed loans to the private sector that are insufficiently collateralized should be transferred to the federal balance sheet. While the Fed cannot go bankrupt, any Fed losses are ultimately borne by U.S. taxpayers and should be directly and transparently accounted for as part of the federal budget. For the same reason, in the future, only the Treasury should engage in insufficiently collateralized lending.

But rather than reinforcing the Fed's independence, as our proposal would do, the Obama administration urges amending Section 13(3) to require the written approval of the secretary of the Treasury for any emergency extension of credit. This expansion of Treasury power over the Fed's use of liquidity facilities in classic lender of last resort situations—that is, where there was adequate collateral—is startling and unwise. Instead, the lines of authority should be clear. The Fed should have strengthened authority to loan against adequate collateral in an emergency. And the Fed should have no authority, even with the approval of the Treasury, to loan against insufficient collateral.

The Fed needs authority to lend in a crisis to avoid the chain reaction of failures of financial institutions, which could result in a complete economic collapse. However, this reason to act should not jeopardize the Fed's credibility and independence. Instead, these goals can be achieved by giving the Fed full authority to lend against good collateral—a traditional power of a central bank—while requiring bailouts to be undertaken by the government. This change will enhance both the Fed's credibility and its independence and make our government more accountable.

TIME TO ACT

The Dodd-Frank Act missed a major opportunity for financial regulatory reform. The time for real financial regulatory reform is now. But now is also the time for serious thinking and analysis, not knee-jerk responses. A clear road map for reducing systemic risk, enhancing transparency, and modernizing regulatory institutions is the better medicine.

NOTES

1. Committee on Capital Markets Regulation, www.capmktsreg .org.
2. Committee on Capital Markets Regulation, "Recommendations for Reorganizing the U.S. Regulatory Structure," January 14, 2009. Available at www.capmktsreg.org/pdfs/01.14.09_CCMR_Recommenda tions_for_Reorganizing_the_US_Regulatory_Structure.pdf.

CHAPTER 11

A Recipe for Ratings Reform

Charles W. Calomiris

CREDIT RATING AGENCIES such as Moody's, Standard and Poor's, and Fitch used to be bit players in the dramas that attend financial crises. No more. Recent hearings at the House Committee for Oversight and Government Reform provided the latest in a series of surprising spectacles about the agencies, this time in accusatory exchanges among former and current executives of Moody's. And new controversies are brewing: the engineering of a new set of complex transactions called "re-remics," where rating agencies help repackage securities on a bank or an insurance company's balance sheet to achieve an improvement of the ratings of the portfolios.

What is the evidence that rating agencies performed badly in measuring credit risk on the debts that they rate? Were rating agencies suborned, and, if so, by whom and to what purpose?

The evidence of rating agency failure shows up in *inflated* ratings and *low-quality* ratings. The inflation of ratings is the purposeful underestimation of default risk on rated debts. Low-quality ratings

Charles W. Calomiris is the Henry Kaufman Professor of Financial Institutions at Columbia Business School.

are ratings based on flawed measures of underlying risk. The recent collapse of subprime-related securitizations revealed both problems in the extreme.

What harm do these deficiencies do? Inflation subverts the intent of regulations that use ratings to control risk-taking, resulting in ineffectual prudential regulation. If rating inflation is accompanied by low-quality ratings, this causes deeper problems. Investors can "reverse engineer" a debt rating that is merely inflated and recover the true measure of risk; the revelation of severe flaws in risk modeling that usually occur in response to a financial shock leaves investors unsure of how to price the debts they are holding and unwilling to buy additional debts of similar securitizations, resulting in severe market disruption.

Evidence abounds that severe errors in subprime ratings were predictable. The two most important modeling errors relating to subprime risk were both assumptions that contradicted logic and experience, namely, that U.S. house prices could not decline, and that the underwriting of no-docs mortgages would not lead to a severe deterioration in borrower quality.

THE SOURCE OF THE PROBLEM

Who was behind these biased models? Many policy makers incorrectly believe that securitization sponsors are the constituency that control ratings. That is false. Ratings that exaggerated the quality of securitized debts were demanded by the *buy* side of the market (the institutional investors whose portfolio purchases are being regulated according to the ratings that are attached to those purchases) because inflated ratings benefited them. Why?

Ratings that understate risk are helpful to institutional investors because they (1) increase institutional investors' flexibility in investing, (2) reduce the amount of capital institutions have to maintain against their investments (the objective of re-remics alchemy), and (3) increase their perceived risk-adjusted profitability in the eyes of less sophisticated ultimate investors (mutual fund, bank, and insurance company shareholders, pensioners, or policyholders) by making it appear that an AAA-rated investment is earning an AA-rated return. If buyers wish rating agencies to inflate ratings to overcome regulatory hurdles and make them appear more favorably in the eyes of their ultimate investors, rating agencies can reap substantial profits from catering to buyers' demands for inflated ratings. This has an important implication: rating inflation on securitized debts is done at the behest of the *buy side*.

Consider the case of the collateralized debt obligation (CDO) market. CDOs were constructed using unsold debts from other securitizations (often subprime mortgage-backed securities [MBS]). CDO issuance volume increased dramatically in the early 2000s, rising from $100–150 billion a year in the period 1998–2004 to $250 billion in 2005 and $500 billion in 2006.

Were institutional investors aware of the high risk of CDOs prior to the 2006 boom? Yes. Moody's published data on the five-year probability of default, as of December 2005, for Baa CDO tranches of CDOs, which showed that these Baa debts had a 20 percent five-year probability of default, in contrast to the Baa corporate debts, which showed only a 2 percent five-year probability of default. Despite the rhetoric that rating agencies publish claiming to maintain uniformity in rating scales, institutional investors knew better: in 2005, CDO debts of a given rating were ten times as risky as similarly rated corporate debts.

Why did institutional investors play this game? Asset managers were placing someone else's money at risk and earning huge salaries, bonuses, and management fees for being willing to pretend that these were reasonable investments. On one occasion, when one agency was uninvited by a sponsor from providing a rating (because the rating agency did not offer to approve as high a percentage limit for AAA debt as the other agencies), that agency warned a prominent institutional investor not to participate as a buyer but was rebuffed with the statement: "We have to put our money to work."

Rating agencies gave legitimacy to this pretense, and were paid to do so. Investors may have reasoned that others were behaving similarly, and that all were protected by the biased models of risk. The script would be clear and would give plausible deniability to all involved. "Who knew? We all thought that the model gave the right loss assumption! That was what the rating agencies used."

Strong evidence that buy-side investors encouraged the debasement of the ratings process comes from the phenomenon of "ratings shopping." Before actually requesting that a rating agency rate something, sponsors ask rating agencies to tell them, hypothetically, how much AAA debt they would allow to be issued against a given pool of securities being put into the CDO portfolio. If a rating agency gives too conservative an answer relative to its competitors, the sponsor just uses another rating agency.

HOW TO STOP A RACE TO THE BOTTOM

It is crucial to recognize, however, that for ratings shopping to result in a race to the bottom in ratings, the race to the bottom must be welcomed by the buyers; if institutional investors punish the absence of a relatively good agency's rating of an offering (by refusing to buy or paying a sufficiently lower price), then would-be ratings shoppers would have no incentive to exclude reputable rating agencies. Thus the evidence that ratings shopping tends to produce a race to the bottom implies that the buy side favors the low-quality, inflated ratings that result from the race to the bottom.

Under pressure from Fitch, Congress and the Securities and Exchange Commission (SEC) also played a role in encouraging the debasement of ratings of subprime MBS and related securities. Congress passed legislation in 2006 that prodded the SEC to propose "anti-notching" regulations that would have facilitated ratings shopping in the subprime MBS market. "Notching" arose when CDO sponsors brought a pool of securities to a rating agency to be rated, which included debts (often subprime MBS) not previously rated by that rating agency. When asked to rate the CDO that contained those subprime MBS, Moody's, say, would offer either to rate the underlying MBS from scratch, or to notch (adjust by ratings downgrades) the ratings that had been given by, say, Fitch.

The new rules would have forced each rating agency to accept ratings of other agencies without adjustment when rating CDO pools. Even though the anti-notching regulations were still being considered at the time the crisis broke out, the legislation and proposed regulations sent a strong signal to the rating industry. It is quite possible (based on my discussions with insiders) that it had an effect on rating agencies' practices in rating subprime MBS as early as 2006. This policy constituted an attack on any remaining conservatism within the ratings industry: trying to swim against the tide of ratings inflation would put a rating agency at risk of running afoul of its regulator!

WHAT WILL WORK

Once one recognizes that the core constituency for low-quality and inflated ratings is the buy side in the securitized debt market, that carries important implications for reform. Proposals that would require buy-side investors to pay for ratings, rather than the current practice of having securitization sponsors pay for ratings, would have no effect in improving ratings.

The elimination of the use of ratings for regulatory purposes would remove some of the incentive for ratings inflation, but, by itself, this would not solve the problem of inflated and low-quality ratings, since the buy-side agency problem would continue to generate a demand for inflated, low-quality ratings in the securitization markets, where incentive-conflicted institutional investors dominate.

Any solution to the problem *must make it profitable for rating agencies to issue high-quality, non-inflated ratings*, notwithstanding the demand for low-quality, inflated ratings by institutional investors. This can only be accomplished by objectifying the meaning of ratings and linking fees earned by rating agencies to their performance. If fees are linked to the quality of objectified ratings, then ratings agencies would find it unprofitable to cater to buy-side preferences for inflated, low-quality ratings. How could this be done?

All agencies wishing to qualify as Nationally Recognized Statistical Rating Organizations (NRSROs)—the rating agencies whose ratings are used in regulation—would be required to submit ratings for regulatory purposes that link letter grades to estimates of the probability of default and the expected loss given default. Once the ratings are presented as numbers, rating agencies could be held accountable for their ratings. For example, if an NRSRO's ratings for a particular product were found to be persistently inflated, then it would face a penalty. That penalty could "claw back" fees the agency had earned on that product (enforced by requiring that agencies post some of their fees as a "bond" to draw upon). Alternatively, a rating agency found to have exaggerated its ratings could simply lose its NRSRO status for a brief time (say, several months), which would also provide powerful incentives not to inflate.

REFERENCES AND FURTHER READING

Bloomberg Markets magazine, July 2007.
Calomiris, Charles. 2009. "The Debasement of Ratings: What's Wrong and How We Can Fix It." e21, October 26. Available at www.eco nomics21.org/content/2the-debasement-ratings-whats-wrong-and -how-we-can-fix-it.

CHAPTER 12

Should Banker Pay Be Regulated?

Steven N. Kaplan

IN THE AFTERMATH of last year's banking crisis, world leaders are looking for ways to see that this never happens again. G-20 leaders, the Obama administration, and, apparently, the Federal Reserve have focused on pay practices at financial firms as being a key cause of the recent disaster and have proposed restricting bankers' pay. These restrictions largely amount to reducing short-term cash bonus payouts, increasing the use of restricted stock and options, and requiring the executives to hold the restricted stock and options for a period longer than the usual four-year vesting period. The big question is: "Will it work?"

IS PAY THE ROOT OF ALL EVIL?

Before instituting what is likely to be a quite invasive regulatory system, perhaps we should take a closer look to see if past pay structures

Steven N. Kaplan is the Neubauer Family Professor of Entrepreneurship and Finance at the University of Chicago Booth School of Business.

really were at the heart of our recent problems. The poor pay practice explanation for the crisis implies the following:

1. Top bank executives were rewarded for short-term results with large amounts of up-front cash pay.
2. Bank executives did not hold sufficiently large amounts of stock to align their interests with those of shareholders.
3. Executives with more short-term pay and less stock ownership should have had the greatest incentive to take bad and excessive risks and, so, should have performed worst in the crisis.

In recent work, Rudiger Fahlenbrach and Rene Stulz (2009) test these implications by studying the CEOs of almost one hundred large financial institutions from 2006 to 2008. They start in 2006 because that is a good candidate for the point at which financial firms took on the risky positions that led to the crisis.

In 2006 the mean CEO took home $3.6 million in cash compensation, which represented less than half of total compensation. The larger share of pay was in restricted stock and options. At the same time, the mean CEO held $88 million worth of the firm's equity and options. In other words, the CEO took home $3.6 million in cash, on average, while leaving more than twenty-four times as much in his or her firm. It seems unlikely that the up-front cash pay provided much of an incentive for the average CEO to knowingly take bad or excessive risks that would jeopardize his or her much larger equity stakes.

Consistent with this conclusion, CEOs lost a lot in the crisis. From 2006 to 2008, the average CEO lost $31 million in his or her holdings of the firm's stock, again, dwarfing any gains from cash compensation. The CEOs lost large amounts on their options as well.

Finally, and again in contrast to the excessive risk assumption, Fahlenbrach and Stulz do not find that, for banks, CEOs with less equity generated worse stock performance. If anything, bank CEOs with more equity had worse performance.

These results led Fahlenbrach and Stulz (2009) to conclude that bank "CEO incentives cannot be blamed for the credit crisis or for the performance of banks during that crisis."

David Yermack (2009) points out that many prominent financial executives lost "small fortunes" in 2008. He adds that "farther down the ladder, most mid- and upper-level managers of financial companies also lost a significant amount of their net worth in 2008."

Yermack concludes that "the recent scrutiny of executive pay seems to stem from an odd mix of envy and vengeance, unsupported by facts or theories." Yermack, a noted researcher on CEO pay, has written several articles highly critical of specific CEO compensation practices—such as corporate jet usage. Nevertheless, his conclusion on the relation of CEO pay to the financial crisis is diametrically opposed to those of advocates for tight pay regulation.

Ing-Haw Cheng, Harrison Hong, and Jose Scheinkman (2009) find some evidence consistent with the story of short-termism leading to excessive risk. They find that financial firms that paid higher total compensation relative to their size had modestly higher stock volatility and significantly lower stock returns from 2001 to 2008.

Their results, however, are largely driven by insurance firms. With insurance firms excluded, their results are only marginally economically and statistically significant. They do not point to compensation as a major cause of the crisis.

Furthermore, the specific pay restrictions under consideration—dramatically increasing the period between the time stock compensation is issued and the time it can be sold—would not have stopped the longer-serving executives like Cayne of Bear Stearns, Fuld of Lehman, and Lewis of Bank of America from selling their shares before the crisis. These executives received large amounts of stock and options in the 1990s, essentially all of which would have been eligible for sale under most of the proposed plans.

If front-loaded incentives were not the reason that bank CEOs got in this mess, what did cause the crisis? John Taylor (2009) points to highly expansionary monetary policy in the years leading up to the crisis. Douglas Diamond and Raghuram Rajan (2009) cite the so-called capital glut—large inflows of external capital from China and much of the developing world. Charles Calomiris (2009) highlights the role of the political system in inflating the banking sector and real estate prices, particularly the subprime sector, through low-income housing mandates implemented by Fannie Mae, Freddie Mac, and others. Ruling out compensation practices hardly leaves us at a loss for culprits in the recent debacle.

Perhaps the following episode can also provide some insight. A well-known partnership, led by a charismatic CEO, raised outside capital to fund a new investment vehicle. The partnership put up 10 percent of the money in the investment vehicle. That 10 percent represented 50 percent of the partnership's capital. Most of the partners' net worth was invested in the partnership, so the partners had substantial "skin in the game." And the partners did not take large fees or any other meaningful short-term compensation out of the partnership, completely in line with the current recommendations for pay reform.

Unfortunately, the partners leveraged the first investment vehicle by investing in a second and third vehicle. Then the stock market declined substantially, almost bankrupting the partnership.

The partnership was Goldman Sachs in the late 1920s and early 1930s. The investment vehicle was the Goldman Sachs Trading Corporation. It took Goldman more than twenty years to recover its capital. When asked to explain why Goldman had made such a risky bet, Walter Sachs did not mention compensation. Instead, he simply responded, "to conquer the world" (Endlich 1999).

The point of the Goldman Sachs example is that restrictions on pay are not necessarily effective in the face of a bull market and the subsequent crisis. One suspects they also are ineffective in stopping CEOs who want "to conquer the world."

THE DOWNSIDE TO PAY REGULATION

While the proposed pay restrictions are unlikely to stop the next financial crisis, they are likely to damage the financial sector. To see why, it is important to understand why bankers are paid so much.

Over the last two to three decades, technological change and increased scale have led to much greater productivity and much higher incomes for those at the top of the income distribution. Corporate executives manage larger companies. Investors manage much larger sums of money. Entertainers and athletes access larger audiences. Lawyers oversee larger transactions and larger cases. Joshua Rauh and I (see Kaplan and Rauh 2009) have found that pay for all of these groups has increased much more than pay for the average worker.

Given this reality, the best bankers, traders, deal makers, and so on will work for the companies that are able to provide the most attractive compensation packages. Greater pay regulation will drive more of the most talented away from regulated banks and toward hedge funds, private equity funds, boutique investment banks, and other unregulated investment firms. We have already seen top talent leave AIG and other Troubled Asset Relief Program (TARP)-constrained institutions.

The potential talent drain is likely to be exacerbated as pay regulations impose a one-size-fits-all regime on all bank employees. Why impose restrictions on a deal maker who earns a large fee for putting a merger together that does not impose any risk on the bank after the transaction has closed? The same is true for a trader who makes money on spreads rather than from taking on risk. These types of employees will be penalized for no good end under the proposed pay regimes.

Perhaps more troubling is that pay restrictions open up a Pandora's box of other restrictions. As Professor Bebchuk (2009) has admitted elsewhere, politicians are often more interested in setting limits to total compensation than in designing the optimal form of compensation. Demagogic politicians believe such restrictions make them look good in the eyes of angry voters.

We saw this earlier in 2009 when restrictions on total pay at TARP recipients were inserted in an unrelated bill as part of the Obama stimulus package. And we see this in the pay packages recently imposed by the Obama administration pay czar at AIG, Citigroup, and Bank of America. Gabriel Sherman (2009) reports that Feinberg's decisions on pay levels were explicitly motivated by political considerations. It is naïve for Bebchuk to argue that only pay structures will be regulated, not pay levels.

One might also worry that the financial sector will move increasingly to a Fannie-Freddie style arrangement in which banks use their capital to advance the pet projects and political fortunes of lawmakers in exchange for lawmakers guaranteeing sympathetic regulatory treatment.

A BETTER SOLUTION

Banks have a special function in the economy that does warrant a special role for the government: not in setting pay but in imposing effective capital requirements. A better solution would impose higher and pro-cyclical equity capital requirements on banks combined with a requirement to raise contingent long-term debt—debt that converts into equity in a crisis.

Banks would be required to have some minimum amount of equity capital, say 10 percent of total capital—much like current requirements. Investment banks like Bear Stearns and Lehman got into trouble because they had too little equity capital—far less than 10 percent. Regulators might consider imposing pro-cyclical equity requirements—increasing the equity percentage in boom times in order to offset losses in the inevitable bust times.

In addition, regulators would require banks to issue an additional amount of capital—say, 10 percent—in the form of long-term debt that is forced to convert into equity if the bank and the overall banking system get into financial difficulty.

Lloyds recently issued such contingent capital bonds. The bonds automatically convert into a predetermined amount of equity if Lloyd's tier-1 equity capital falls below 5 percent of assets. Although Lloyd's did not do so, one might add a systemic trigger, that is, the bonds do not convert unless the banking system as a whole also has seen a decline in equity capital.

Banks will have to pay a higher interest rate on contingent capital bonds than on straight long-term debt, since debt investors will face the true cost of capital, not the government subsidized one. Over time, however, the extra interest rate is likely to be small, as the imposition of higher capital requirements and contingent capital will significantly reduce the likelihood of ever reaching the triggers.

Bankruptcy is a terribly messy process for large financial firms with stakes in a variety of complex transactions, operating in multiple jurisdictions. If this contingent capital structure had been in place before the crisis, troubled banks would have been recapitalized with the capital of the contingent debt holders while avoiding the delays, complications, and legal posturing that are inevitable in the formal bankruptcy process. These debt investors, not the government, would have bailed out the banks and investment banks. The financial crisis would have been substantially smaller, if it had occurred at all. Contingent capital and pro-cyclical equity requirements are also effective in reducing the potential damage done by financial sector firms that want to conquer the world.

REFERENCES AND FURTHER READING

Bebchuk, Lucian. 2009. "Fixing Banker's Pay." *The Economist's Voice* 6, no. 11: art. 7. Available at www.bepress.com/ev/vol6/iss11/art7.

Calomiris, Charles. 2009. "Banking Crises and the Rules of the Game." NBER Working Paper No. 15403. Available at www.nber.org/papers /w15403.

Cheng, Ing-Haw, Harrison Hong, and Jose Scheinkman. 2009. "Yesterday's Heroes: Compensation and Creative Risk-Taking." Working Paper, Princeton University. Available at www.princeton.edu/~joses /wp/yesterday.pdf.

Diamond, Douglas W., and Raghuram Rajan. 2009. "The Credit Crisis: Conjectures About Causes and Remedies." NBER Working Paper No. 14739. Available at www.nber.org/papers/w14739.

Endlich, Lisa. 1999. *Goldman Sachs: The Culture of Success*. New York: Alfred A. Knopf.

Fahlenbrach, R., and R. Stulz. 2009. "Bank CEO Incentives and the Credit Crisis." Working Paper, Ohio State University. Available at www.nber.org/papers/w15212.

Kaplan, Steven, and J. Rauh. 2009. "Wall Street and Main Street: What Contributes to the Rise in the Highest Incomes?" *Review of Financial Studies* 23, no. 3.

Sherman, Gabriel. 2009. "Show Me the Money." *New York Magazine*, November 22. Available at http://nymag.com/news/business/62259.

Taylor, John. 2009. "The Financial Crisis and the Policy Responses: An Empirical Analysis of What Went Wrong." NBER Working Paper No. 14631. Available at www.nber.org/papers/w14631.

Yermack, D. 2009. "Keeping the Pay Police at Bay." *Wall Street Journal*, October 10. Available at http://online.wsj.com/article/SB1000142405 27487037466045744614625981264 06.html.

CHAPTER 13

Fixing Bankers' Pay

Lucian A. Bebchuk

IN THE AFTERMATH of the financial crisis of 2008–2009, there are widespread concerns that the compensation structures of financial firms have provided excessive risk-taking incentives. Responding to such concerns, firms are seeking to reform their pay packages to avoid such incentives, and regulators around the world are moving toward setting standards for compensation structures in financial firms. The G-20 leaders, in their September 2009 summit, announced their commitment "to implement strong international compensation standards aimed at ending practices that lead to excessive risk-taking," and the Federal Reserve Board in October 2009 requested comments on a "proposed guidance" that contemplates scrutiny of compensation structures by banking supervisors.

I have been for some time an advocate of such reform and regulation of financial firms' compensation structures, making the case in

Lucian A. Bebchuk is Professor of Law, Economics, and Finance and Director of the Program on Corporate Governance at Harvard Law School. Although Bebchuk serves as a consultant to the Special Master for TARP Executive Compensation in the U.S. Treasury, the views expressed in this chapter do not necessarily reflect the views of the Office of the Special Master or any other individual affiliated with it.

academic articles, congressional testimony, and a series of op-ed articles listed in this chapter's references. In what follows I attempt to synthesize this body of writing and provide a brief statement of the normative case for regulation of pay in financial firms, the relationship between such regulation and the standard prudential regulation of finance, and what financial regulators should do in this area.

Before proceeding to discuss the role of the government in this area, I begin by describing two distinct sources of risk-taking incentives—two ways in which banks' standard pay arrangements have insulated their executives from part of the downside of risks they take. (By "banks" I refer throughout to any financial institutions that are deemed to pose systemic risk and are therefore subject to prudential regulation.) I also analyze how compensation structures can best be redesigned to address these problems. If financial regulators indeed begin to monitor and regulate pay arrangements, they would do well to focus on the design flaws and design solutions discussed here.

INSULATION FROM LONG-TERM LOSSES TO SHAREHOLDERS

Much attention is now focused on the fact that pay arrangements have provided executives with incentives to focus on short-term results. This problem, first highlighted in a book (see Bebchuk and Fried 2004) and accompanying articles that Jesse Fried and I published five years ago, has recently become widely recognized—including by business leaders such as the CEO of Goldman Sachs.

Standard pay arrangements reward executives for short-term results even when these results are subsequently reversed. The ability to take a large amount of compensation based on short-term results off the table provides executives with incentives to seek short-term gains even when these come at the expense of long-term value, or even at the risk of an implosion later on.

Under the standard design of equity-based compensation, stock options and restricted shares vest gradually over a period of time. Once options and shares vest, however, executives typically have unrestricted freedom to cash them out, and often unload such equity incentives quickly after vesting. This broad freedom to cash out equity incentives has contributed substantially to creating short-term distortions.

To address these distortions, it is desirable to separate the time that options and restricted shares can be cashed out from the time in which they vest, as Jesse Fried and I proposed in *Pay Without Performance* (Bebchuk and Fried 2004). As soon as an executive has completed an additional year at the firm, the options or shares promised as compensation for that year's work should vest and should belong to the executive even if he or she immediately leaves the firm. But the cashing out of these vested options and shares should be "blocked" for a specified period after vesting—the executive should be allowed to cash them out only down the road.

Some shareholder proposals and compensation experts have called for allowing executives to cash out shares and options only upon retirement from the firm. Such a "hold-till-retirement" requirement, however, would provide executives with a counterproductive incentive to *leave* the firm in order to cash out their portfolio of options and shares and diversify their risks. Perversely, the incentive to leave will be strongest for executives who have served successfully for a long time and whose accumulated options and shares are especially valuable. Similar distortions arise under any arrangement tying the freedom to cash out to an event that is at least partly under an executive's control.

To avoid the above problems, the period during which the vested options and shares are "blocked" and may not be cashed out should be fixed. For example, when options or shares of an executive vest in a given year of employment, they could become unblocked, and the executive would subsequently be free to cash them out on the seventh-year anniversary of the vesting. Because the executive can't accelerate the time of cashing out, this arrangement doesn't provide distorted incentives arising from the desire to obtain such acceleration. And as long as an executive is working for the firm and accruing options and shares that continue to vest, he or she will always have an incentive to care about the company's long-term share value.

Bonus compensation also needs to be redesigned. Under standard pay arrangements, executives have been able to cash bonus compensation based on short-term results and keep it even when those results were subsequently reversed. To address the short-term distortion arising from such arrangements, bonuses should not be cashed right away, but instead placed in a company account for several years and adjusted downward if the company subsequently learns that the reasons for the bonus no longer hold up.

INSULATION FROM LOSSES TO CAPITAL SUPPLIERS OTHER THAN SHAREHOLDERS

Thus far I have focused on the insulation of executives from long-terms losses to shareholders—the problem that has received most attention following the current crisis. However, as Holger Spamann and I analyze in detail in recent work (see Bebchuk and Spamann 2009a, b), there is another type of distortion that should be recognized. The payoffs of financial executives have been insulated from the consequences that losses could impose on parties other than shareholders. This source of distortion is separate and distinct from the "short-termism" problem discussed above and would remain even if executives' payoffs were fully aligned with those of long-term shareholders.

Equity-based awards, coupled with the capital structure of banks, tie executives' compensation to a highly levered bet on the value of banks' assets. Bank executives expect to share in any gains that might flow to common shareholders, but they are insulated from losses that the realization of risks could impose on preferred shareholders, bondholders, depositors, or the government as a guarantor of deposits. This causes executives to pay insufficient attention to the possibility of large losses and therefore provides them with incentives to take excessive risks.

How could pay arrangements be redesigned to address this distortion? To the extent that executive pay is tied to the value of specified securities, such pay could be tied to a broader basket of securities, not only common shares. Thus, rather than tying executive pay to a specified percentage of the value of the common shares of the bank holding company, compensation could be tied to a specified percentage of the aggregate value of the common shares, the preferred shares, and all the outstanding bonds issued by either the bank holding company or the bank. Because such a compensation structure would expose executives to a broader fraction of the negative consequences of risks taken, it would reduce their incentives to take excessive risks.

Even the structure described above would cause bank executives to internalize fully the adverse consequences that risk-taking might have for the interests of the government as guarantor of deposits. To achieve that would require broadening further the set of positions to whose aggregate value executive payoffs are tied. One could consider, for example, schemes in which executive payoffs are tied not to a given percentage of the aggregate value of the bank's common shares, preferred shares, and bonds at a specified point in time, but rather to this aggregate value minus any payments made by the government to the bank's depositors, as well as other payments made by the government in support of the bank, during the period ending at the specified time.

Alternatively, one could consider tying executive payoffs to the aggregate value of the bank's common shares, preferred shares, and bonds at the specified time minus the expected value of future government payments as proxied by the product of (1) the implied probability of default inferred from the price of credit default swaps at the specified time, and (2) the value of the bank's deposits at that time. Even if such schemes are not used, however, tying executive pay to the aggregate value of common shares, preferred shares, and bonds will by itself produce a significant improvement in incentives compared with existing arrangements.

Similarly, to the extent that executives receive bonus compensation tied to specified accounting measures, it could be tied instead to broader measures. For example, the bonus compensation of some bank executives has been based on accounting measures that are of interest primarily to common shareholders, such as return on equity or earning per common share. It would be worthwhile to consider basing bonus compensation instead on broader measures, such as earnings before any payments made to bondholders.

THE ROLE OF GOVERNMENT

Having discussed what changes in pay arrangements would curtail incentives to take excessive risks in banks as well as in other firms, I turn to the question of what role, if any, the government should play in bringing about such changes. Some would argue that, even accepting the desirability of significant changes, making such changes should be left to unconstrained choices by private decision makers and that, at least for firms not receiving public funding, the government should not play any role in the setting of executive compensation.

For public firms outside the financial sector, the government should indeed avoid setting any limits on the compensation structures from which private decision makers may choose. For such firms, the government should focus solely on improving internal governance processes, and then not intervene in the substantive choices made by shareholders and the directors elected by them.

Some may suggest that government intervention to ensure the adequacy of internal governance processes would be sufficient also in the financial sector. And authorities around the world have been paying increased attention to improving governance in financial firms. The Basel committee of bank supervisors has been stressing the importance of involving banks' boards in pay setting, and the U.S. House of Representatives, with support from the Obama administration, passed legislation that would introduce say-on-pay votes and bolster the independence of compensation committees.

As is the case for non-financial firms, the government should indeed seek to improve the internal governance and pay-setting processes within banks. In the case of banks, however, the government's role should go beyond governance reforms. Because of the special circumstances of financial firms, financial regulators should monitor and regulate compensation structures. Such pay regulation is justified by the same moral hazard reasons that underlie the long-standing system of prudential regulation of banks.

PAY REGULATION AND PRUDENTIAL REGULATION

When a bank takes risks, shareholders can expect to capture the full upside, but part of the downside may be borne by the government as guarantor of deposits. Because bank failure will impose costs on the government and the economy that shareholders do not internalize, shareholders' interests would be served by more risk-taking than would be in the interest of the government and the economy. This moral hazard problem provides a basis for the extensive body of regulations that restrict the choices of financial firms with respect to investments, lending, and capital reserves.

Curtailing agency problems between executives and shareholders, which governance reforms seek to do, could eliminate risk-taking that is excessive even from the shareholders' perspective. But it cannot be expected to eliminate incentives for risk-taking that are excessive from a social perspective but not from the perspective of shareholders.

Shareholders' interest in more risk-taking implies that they could benefit from providing bank executives with incentives to take excessive risks. Executives with such incentives could use their informational advantages and whatever discretion traditional regulations leave them to further increase risks. Given the complexities of modern finance and the limited information and resources of regulators, the traditional regulation of banks' actions and activities is necessarily imperfect. Thus when executives have incentives to do so, they may be able to take risks beyond what is intended or assumed by the regulators, who may often be one step behind banks' executives.

Because shareholders' interests favor incentives for risk-taking that are excessive from a social perspective, substantive regulation of the terms of pay arrangements—limiting the use of structures that reward excessive risk-taking—can advance the goals of banking regulation. The regulators' focus should be on the *structure* of compensation—not the amount—with the aim of discouraging the taking of excessive risks. By doing so, regulators would induce bank executives to work for, not against, the goals of banking regulation.

The regulation of bankers' pay could nicely supplement and reinforce the traditional, direct regulation of banks' activities. Indeed, if pay arrangements are designed to discourage excessive risk-taking, direct regulation of activities could be less tight than it should otherwise be. Conversely, as long as banks' executive pay arrangements are unconstrained, regulators should be stricter in their monitoring and direct regulation of banks' activities.

At a minimum, when assessing the risks posed by any given bank, regulators should take into account the incentives generated by the bank's pay arrangements. When pay arrangements encourage risk-taking, regulators should monitor the bank more closely and should consider raising its capital requirements.

OBJECTIONS

(1) It's the Shareholders' Money. Pay regulation in banks could be opposed on grounds that the government does not have a legitimate interest in telling bank shareholders how to spend their money. Choices of compensation structures, it might be argued, inherently belong to the province of private business decisions where regulators should not trespass. This objection is not persuasive, however, because the government does have a legitimate interest in the compensation structures of private financial firms. Given the government's interest in the safety and soundness of banks, its intervention here will be as legitimate as the traditional forms of intervention that limit banks' investment and lending decisions.

(2) Regulators Know Less. Opponents of regulating executive pay in banks could also argue that regulators will be at an informational disadvantage when setting pay arrangements. But placing limits on compensation structures that incentivize risk-taking would be no more demanding in terms of information than regulators' direct intervention in investment, lending, and capital decisions. Furthermore, the setting of pay arrangements should not be left to the unconstrained choices of informed players inside banks because such players do not have incentives to take into account the interests of bondholders, depositors, and the government in setting pay.

(3) Bankers Will Flee. Opponents may also argue that pay regulation will drive talent away and that financial firms will lose valuable employees. As I stressed, however, regulation of pay in financial firms should focus on pay structures and should not limit compensation levels. (Prudential regulation may, of course, impose such limits to the extent that compensation level might result in cash outflows that would leave the bank with insufficient capital.) Indeed, the bill passed by the House of Representatives, and the Federal Reserve Board's proposed guidance, explicitly rules out intervention in pay levels.

Thus to the extent that the use of pay structures that eliminate perverse incentives would be less attractive to some executives, banks would be able to compensate those executives with higher levels of expected pay. Even when such an increase proved necessary, however, providing more efficient incentives would be worthwhile.

(4) Regulatory Abuse. Finally, some opponents may worry that pay regulation would provide regulators with increased power that they might sometimes abuse. Regulators might use their power to advance political objectives, it might be argued, and banks might respond by increasing their investments in political contributions and their efforts to curry favor with the political establishment. However, banking regulators already wield vast powers over banks—and, as long as the existing banking system with its moral hazard problems is retained, such powers appear unavoidable. Indeed, as the Federal Reserve Board's proposed guidance makes clear, banking regulators' power to protect the safety and soundness of the banking system *has* long provided them with the authority to limit pay arrangements that induce excessive risk-taking—authority that they elected not to use in the past. The main effect of the approach I support thus would not make regulators markedly more powerful but rather encourage them to expand their toolkit and thereby improve their ability to guard financial stability.

GOING FORWARD

Compensation structures for financial executives should be redesigned in the ways discussed above to avoid the excessive incentives for risk-taking that standard pay arrangements have provided in the past. Regulators have a role in ensuring that such changes take place. Monitoring and regulating the compensation structures of bank executives should be an important instrument in the toolkit of financial regulators.

REFERENCES AND FURTHER READING

Bebchuk, Lucian. 2009a. "Paying for Performance at Goldman." *Wall Street Journal Online,* July 24. Available at http://online.wsj.com /article/SB124838248270177043.html.

Bebchuk, Lucian. 2009b. "Regulate Financial Pay to Reduce Risk-Taking." *Financial Times,* August 3. Available at www.ft.com/cms/s/0 /e34d6d4e-8058–11de-bf04–00144feabdc0.html?nclick_check=1.

Bebchuk, Lucian. 2009c. "Why Financial Pay Shouldn't Be Left to the Market." Project Syndicate, August. Available at www.projectsyndi cate.org/commentary/bebchuk4.

Bebchuk, Lucian. 2009d. "Written Testimony, Hearing on Compensation Structures and Systemic Risk, June 11." Committee on Financial Services, U.S. House of Representatives. Available at www .house.gov/apps/list/hearing/financialsvcs_dem/bebchuk.pdf.

Bebchuk, Lucian, and Alma Cohen. 2009. "Back to the Good Times on Wall Street." *Wall Street Journal Online,* July 31. Available at http:// blogs.wsj.com/economics/2009/07/31/guestcontribution-back-to -the-good-times-on-wallstreet.

Bebchuk, Lucian, Alma Cohen, and Holger Spamann. 2009. "The Wages of Failure: Executive Compensation at Bear Stearns and Lehman 2000–2008." Working Paper, Harvard Law School.

Bebchuk, Lucian, and Jesse Fried. 2004. *Pay Without Performance.* Cambridge, Mass.: Harvard University Press.

Bebchuk, Lucian, and Jesse Fried. 2009a. "Equity Compensation for Long-Term Performance." Working Paper, Harvard Law School.

Bebchuk, Lucian, and Jesse Fried. 2009b. "Equity Compensation for Long-Term Results." *Wall Street Journal Online,* June 16. Available at http://online.wsj.com/article/SB124516105628518981.html.

Bebchuk, Lucian, and Holger Spamann. 2009a. "Reducing Incentives for Risk-Taking." *New York Times Online,* October 12. Available at http://dealbook.blogs.nytimes.com/2009/10/12/reducing-incentives -for-risktaking.

Bebchuk, Lucian, and Holger Spamann. 2009b. "Regulating Bankers' Pay." Harvard Law School Olin Discussion Paper No. 641. *Georgetown Law Journal.*

Blankfein, Lloyd. 2009. "Do Not Destroy the Essential Catalyst of Risk." *Financial Times,* February 9. Available at www.ft.com/cms/s/0 /0a0f1132-f600–11dd-a9ed-0000779fd2ac.html.

Geithner, Tim. 2009. "Statement of Treasury Secretary Geithner on Compensation." June 10. Available at www.ustreas.gov/press/releases /tg163.htm.

ACKNOWLEDGMENTS

The author would like to thank Alma Cohen, Jesse Fried, and Holger Spamann for joint work on which this chapter draws, and Jonathan Carmel for valuable comments.

CHAPTER 14

It Works for Mergers, Why Not for Finance?

Aaron S. Edlin and Richard J. Gilbert

THE FINANCIAL COLLAPSE that triggered the current great recession has launched a wave of proposals to reform the financial sector to prevent a recurrence. Most, though, are either unlikely to have much of an effect on systemic financial risk or are too complex to be implemented successfully. The Obama administration's "Volker" proposal to limit speculative trading by banks on their own accounts, for example, is well intentioned but a mere Band-Aid. After all, speculation can be done by hedge funds, insurance companies, investment banks, and other financial players, as we learned from Lehman Brothers and the American International Group (AIG). Requiring full disclosure of all financial trades, including derivative contracts, is too complex. The amount of data would overwhelm the resources of existing regulatory

Aaron S. Edlin and Richard J. Gilbert are Professors of Economics at the University of California, Berkeley. During the Clinton administration, Richard Gilbert was Chief Economist at the U.S. Department of Justice and Aaron Edlin was Senior Economist for Antitrust and Regulation at the Council of Economic Advisers.

authorities and would require an operation on the scale of the National Security Agency to analyze.

We propose an intermediate approach that borrows from experience with mergers. The U.S. Department of Justice (DOJ) and the Federal Trade Commission (FTC) review merger activity to detect mergers that may raise prices. Under the Hart-Scott-Rodino Act, all proposed mergers (public or private) that exceed a threshold value must be reported to the FTC. The details of the proposed merger are then reviewed by either the DOJ or the FTC, which can challenge the merger or negotiate modification of its terms.

The system works. In a typical year, the FTC receives about 2,000 to 3,000 merger proposals, of which about 3 percent get a "second look."[1] The other 97 percent proceed without any regulatory oversight. Of the 3 percent that get a second look, the antitrust authorities require some modification prior to approval for roughly half, and they formally object to a small handful.

In evaluating mergers, the antitrust authorities conduct an exhaustive analysis and intervene only when they conclude that a merger is likely to harm consumers. Most economists believe that merger review has benefited the economy.

Why not do something similar for the U.S. financial industry?

A FINANCIAL VERSION OF HART-SCOTT-RODINO

What are the keys to merger oversight by the antitrust agencies? One is that self-reporting is required for all deals over a size threshold. A second is that penalties are sufficient to ensure almost full compliance. And a third is that the substantive standard for review is a general charge, not a long list of specific rules. The general charge is to stop mergers that "may substantially lessen competition," which has come to mean raising prices. The legal standard is as simple as that.

The savings from self-reporting are that the antitrust authorities don't have to find the mergers—the mergers find them. The merging parties must not only identify themselves but must come forward with information about the merger to the authorities and pay a significant fee that can be used to fund the agencies' public interest analysis.

In cases where the agencies are concerned about the merger, they have broad powers of investigation and can ask intrusive questions to understand whether the deal threatens the public interest. For deals that threaten to raise prices, the agencies can sue to block mergers entirely or can pressure the parties to restructure the proposed merger, for example, by spinning off divisions or products.

So what would be the financial analogue? It would be to require detailed reporting of the financial structure and major assets and liabilities for all financial firms whose liabilities exceed some size threshold. For firms over the threshold, regular reporting (likely quarterly) would be required with random audits possible to avoid window dressing before reporting dates.

Instead of intricate and detailed regulations, we would have a standard that avoided firms creating "substantial systemic risk," by which we mean the kind of risk that is likely to cascade through financial markets. The regulator would be charged with making sure these large firms' financial positions do not create undue systemic risks. The regulator would be empowered to require that firms restructure their portfolios, cease taking on more liabilities, raise capital, or even close.

The point of self-reporting is to identify firms worthy of concern, including firms that come from otherwise unregulated or lightly regulated sectors such as insurance and hedge funds. The collapse of AIG is a recent reminder of systemic financial risk but is by no means the first such reminder. The hedge fund Long Term Capital Management, which collapsed in early 2000, had derivative positions valued at about $1.2 trillion,[2] equal to about 15 percent of U.S. GDP at the time. The New York Federal Reserve Bank had to orchestrate a complex unraveling of Long Term's trading positions in order to avoid a potential financial meltdown.

Inspired by merger law, we suggest the general standard of preventing firms from creating "substantial systemic risk," because we believe it is impossible to write specific financial rules in advance that cannot be gamed and that sufficiently anticipate evolving financial instruments and practices. It is better to have a standard like merger law that allows flexibility and evolution with experience.

We focus on liabilities for the threshold because the prospect that liabilities may not be paid in full is inevitably what spawns financial panic. Liabilities should be broadly and generally defined to avoid, as much as possible, being blindsided by derivatives; at the same time it must be recognized that firms may of course have huge liabilities without creating systemic risk, provided that they have appropriate assets to pay the liabilities, or that those to whom they owe the money can bear the loss.

Financial collapse from excessive leverage is a familiar theme, and it is sure to play again in the not too distant future unless something is done (and maybe regardless). Hedge funds and investment banks know that if they can make 10 cents on a $1 trade, then it pays to borrow heavily and earn $100 million on $1 billion in trades, even if they have to pay some interest on the debt. These liabilities are rarely completely hedged, and when the markets change in unexpected ways, the financial system can go into a rapid free fall as counterparties to these trades take actions to contain their risks.

To be sure, the financial industry will be horrified by our proposal. Isn't it intrusive for government to demand that a firm reveal confidential details of its business, let alone be forced to change its risk strategy? Maybe so. But we have long accepted the government's role in mergers, and the government is equally intrusive in gathering information and in requiring spin-offs of divisions or conduct restrictions before blessing a merger. More is surely at stake with systemic financial risk than with mergers, so we should be willing to accept significant loss of business freedom to reduce the risk of financial collapse.

One difference between mergers and financial regulation is that mergers are a distinct event. Once a merger is approved (i.e., not challenged), ongoing monitoring is not needed. Moreover, it seems clean to simply say "no" to a merger, whereas it may appear that financial intervention will involve unscrambling eggs, a difficult task at best.

We think this overstates the differences. Mergers can be challenged after the fact, and firms have been broken up (particularly before Hart-Scott-Rodino). It is true, though, that once a merger is approved, generally the antitrust authorities do not actively monitor the merged firm. Financial regulation must be different in this respect, as very large firms, whether banks or other financial institutions, require ongoing monitoring. Unwinding transactions may be difficult and costly if done quickly, but if monitoring is sufficiently regular, dramatic restructurings will hopefully be unnecessary. In many cases it will be sufficient to tell a firm that it can't take on more of a worrisome risk unless it raises capital that can't flee. And, where more dramatic action is necessary, better sooner than later.

THE DODD BILL

The Dodd bill that emerged from the Senate Banking Committee on March 15 has much in common with our proposal. The bill calls for a new Financial Institutions Regulatory Administration (FIRA) that would be charged with monitoring bank and non-bank companies to guard against systemic risks they may pose for the economy. The bill also empowers FIRA, along with the Federal Deposit Insurance Company, to require financial institutions that pose such risks to adjust or divest certain assets or operations.

We would add to the Dodd bill a self-disclosure requirement akin to merger law. In our view, the severity of the recent financial collapse justifies requiring every financial institution to report its assets and liabilities to the FIRA when its liabilities cross or exceed some threshold. We would also advocate severe penalties for firms that violate the self-disclosure requirement, akin to those in merger law.

Liabilities, like any accounting concept, are ambiguous. Among the challenges for a regulator is to define liabilities in a sufficiently general way to discourage gaming. Firms like Lehman, for example, are now known to have used repurchase agreements to make loans look like sales. Rather than making a specific rule to address that issue, we would urge a general approach in which contracts that are functionally similar to liabilities, or are likely to pose similar risks, be treated as liabilities. Thus, for example, if Long-Term Capital Management entered $1.2 trillion of interest-rate swaps, then, for our purposes, this should count as $1.2 trillion in liabilities backed by $1.2 trillion in assets.

DANGERS OF POLITICS AND CAPTURE

Giving broad powers to a regulator is a scary thing. Government may abuse that power, and politics could interfere with sound decision making. But financial meltdowns scare us more.

The history of merger review and antitrust offers us significant comfort, however (as, by the way, does the history of Federal Reserve independence). Even during its most interventionist period, antitrust never stood significantly in the way of economic progress, and it has rarely been bent for parochial economic interests or partisan political gain.

The exceptions and their rarity prove the rule. Contributions to the Nixon campaign by ITT may have led the Nixon DOJ to be easy on ITT in settling an antitrust case. In fact, that was one of the charges in Nixon's impeachment. Since Nixon, though, there has been a solid wall between the White House and the day-to-day operations of the antitrust division at the DOJ, even though the antitrust chief is a political appointee. In the only case where we know of White House interference, the White House did not fare so well. Bill Baxter, a Reagan political appointee, was in the process of suing AT&T, which he planned to litigate "to the eyeballs." President Reagan called a Cabinet meeting in July 1981 and pointed out in AT&T's defense that when Reagan was young it cost 2 cents to mail a letter cross country and $2 to make a phone call. By the 1980s, each was 20 cents. Baxter, quick as a whip, told Reagan: "Well, Mr. President, when I finish AT&T, I will be happy to take on the Post Office." Baxter proceeded to dismantle AT&T, ignoring politics.[3]

We can't, of course, be sure that politics will be kept at bay, leaving a financial regulator free to protect the economy as best it can, but the antitrust experience gives us some hope.

SUMMING UP

The system works for mergers. It does not require a vast commitment of resources to protect the economy from mergers that might hurt consumers, and firms have become accustomed to the necessity of merger review when they contemplate a major acquisition. The economy deserves the same kind of protection against unbridled financial speculation. Our proposal will offer at least some modest insurance.

NOTES

1. See Federal Trade Commission and Department of Justice 2008.
2. See Edwards 1999, 198.
3. See Areeda, Kaplow, and Edlin 2004, 797.

REFERENCES AND FURTHER READING

Areeda, Phillip, Louis Kaplow, and Aaron Edlin. 2004. *Antitrust Analysis: Problems, Text and Cases*, 6th ed. New York: Aspen Publishers.

Edwards, Franklin R. 1999. "Hedge Funds and the Collapse of Long-Tem Capital Management." *Journal of Economic Perspectives* (Spring): 189–210. Available at www.jstor.org/pss/2647125.

Federal Trade Commission and Department of Justice. 2008. "Hart-Scott-Rodino Annual Report Fiscal Year 2008." Available at www.ftc.gov/os/2009/07/hsrreport.pdf.

U.S. Senate Committee on Banking, Housing, and Urban Affairs. 2009. "Restoring American Financial Stability." Discussion draft. Available at http://banking.senate.gov/public/_files/AYO09D44_xml.pdf.

PART III

FINANCIAL CRISIS
AND BAILOUTS

CHAPTER 15

Hedge Fund Wizards

Dean P. Foster and H. Peyton Young

EVERY OTHER WEEK, it seems, some large hedge fund blows up due to bad bets. Many investors, including supposedly sophisticated ones, are losing their shirts. They shouldn't be surprised, because the deck is stacked against them from the start.

BUYING BLIND

To see how vulnerable investors are in this market, let's imagine for a moment that you are shopping for a "designer" car. These new-fangled vehicles have amazing performance, are manufactured using top-secret methods, and are completely unique. You will never see another one like yours on the road. In shopping for such a vehicle, however, you run into a problem: neither you nor your mechanic is allowed to look under the hood. What's inside is a secret and must

Dean P. Foster is Professor of Statistics at the Wharton School, University of Pennsylvania. H. Peyton Young is the James Meade Professor of Economics at the University of Oxford and a Senior Fellow at the Brookings Institution.

remain so (it's not protected under patent law). Furthermore, you cannot find out how similar vehicles have performed in the past, because there are no similar vehicles. Finally, the vehicle carries no warranty. How much would you pay for such a contraption? Probably not much.

The same logic applies to hedge funds: investors are not allowed to know how they work, every fund is different, and they offer no warranties. In fact, the situation is even worse than this, because it is quite easy for a hedge fund manager to "fake" high performance over an extended period of time without getting caught. It's as if anyone could manufacture a car in his garage that appears turbo-charged initially, but in reality is cobbled together with spare parts and will eventually blow up. Indeed, given this, it may seem surprising that the hedge fund industry has taken off at all.

HIGH PERFORMANCE FROM HIDDEN BAD BETS

To see how high performance can be faked, consider a fairly rare event such as "the S&P 500 will fall by more than 20 percent in the coming year." Events like this are commonly priced in the derivatives market, and they are the staple of many trading strategies. Let's say for the sake of argument that the going price for the S&P event is ten cents on the dollar. In other words, an option on the event costs ten cents now and pays the option-holder a dollar if the event occurs by the end of the year and no money if it does not occur. In effect the market is saying that the probability of this particular event is about 10 percent.

Enter Oz, a strong figure with a smooth manner, a doctorate in physics, and no investment talent. He knows about probabilities, however, and he is running a hedge fund worth $100 million. He decides to write some options on the S&P event and sell them in the marketplace. In order to meet his obligations to the option-holders if the rare event occurs, he parks the $100 million in one-year U.S.

Treasury bills yielding 4 percent. He then sells 100 million covered options, which fetch ten cents on the dollar and thus net $10 million. He takes this $10 million and parks it in Treasury bills too, which enables him to sell another 10 million options. This nets him another $1 million, which he uses to cover incidental expenses.

Oz then takes a long vacation. At the end of the year the probability is 90 percent that his bet has paid off: the rare event does *not* occur, and he owes nothing to the option-holders. In this case the fund grosses $11 million from the sale of the options plus 4 percent on $110 million in Treasury bills, which represents a handsome 15.4 percent return before expenses.

The investors are gratified, and so is Oz. His fee is the standard "two and twenty": 2 percent for funds under management plus a 20 percent performance bonus for returns that exceed some benchmark, say 4 percent. He therefore gets $2 million in management fees plus 20 percent of $11,400,000, which comes to over $4 million gross and over $3 million after expenses. That's good pay for someone with no investment talent. Oz is happy that he left physics.

Oz can then repeat the same gambit next year. Since the rare event only occurs with probability 10 percent in any given year, the probability of a run of good luck is quite high. For example, the chances are nearly 60 percent that the fund will run for more than five years without the rare event occurring, in which case Oz makes over $15 million even if no new money comes to the hedge fund. Better yet, after three straight years of such returns, Oz may find that his modest fund has grown enormously as new investors clamor for a piece of the action.

The trouble is that the investors do not know, and cannot tell, that Oz has no talent. They see the returns given what happened, but not what could have happened. The returns they see look very good and would be very good if the risks were sufficiently low, and Oz assures them they are. Of course, when the rare event *does* occur, and it eventually will, the investors will be cleaned out if they leave their money in the fund. Oz, on the other hand, nets over $3 million in each year before the fund crashes, and much more once news of his early successes gets around.

While most hedge funds probably don't operate in such a nakedly self-serving way, more complex scams of this type probably do take place, as MIT finance professor Andrew Lo has argued (see Lo 2001). Moreover, the outcome for the investors is the same even if managers are honest and merely *think* they can beat the market. Even in our straightforward example, Oz may not be a crook; he may merely *think* that the chance of the S&P tanking is much less than 10 percent.

The bottom line is that hedge fund managers get paid for making bets that put their investors at risk, while taking very little risk themselves. If the fund blows up, the investors cannot tell whether it was due to bad management or just bad luck.

SMALL REGULATORY STEPS

This situation poses some real challenges for regulators. For one thing, such practices are not fraudulent unless one can prove intent. This will be difficult, because the manager can always say he was engaging in arbitrage, that is, he *thought* the odds were better than they turned out to be. Another possibility would be to reform the fee structure. In particular, one might want to penalize underperformance in addition to rewarding high performance in order to discourage excessive risk-taking. Unfortunately, however, any fee structure that rewards true financial wizards also delivers handsome rewards to false wizards, a fact we show in a recent paper (see Foster and Young 2007). Hence, changing the incentives is not going to solve the problem.

It is a conundrum. We do think, though, that some steps toward protecting investors can and should be taken. All hedge funds should be required to register as soon as they are established and to report their returns on a regular basis. Such tracking would allow potential investors to study the records. By itself this would not be enough, as the Oz case shows, but we would be getting somewhere if new rules required managers to keep investors apprised of the fund's downside exposure. Alternatively, managers could guarantee that losses not exceed a certain level, similar to a car manufacturer offering a warranty.

Although individual hedge funds may drag their feet, it is actually in the industry's best interest to encourage greater regulation and transparency. Otherwise, a rising tide of failed funds could cause a collapse in investor confidence, putting both the good and the bad wizards out of business.

REFERENCES AND FURTHER READING

Foster, Dean P., and H. Peyton Young. 2007. "The Hedge Fund Game." Working Paper 07–42, Wharton Financial Institutions Center.

Lo, Andrew W. 2001. "Risk Management for Hedge Funds: Introduction and Overview." *Financial Analysts' Journal* (November–December): 16–33.

CHAPTER 16

Investment Banking Regulation After Bear Stearns

Dwight M. Jaffee and Mark Perlow

IT IS NOW approaching six months since Bear Stearns collapsed and regulators orchestrated a merger by J. P. Morgan that included a $30 billion subsidized loan from the Federal Reserve. The Federal Reserve has, of course, made no promises that it will bail out other investment banks that get into trouble, but there is a widespread perception that it will. Treasury Secretary Paulson, for example, stated on July 31, 2008: "Americans have come to expect the Federal Reserve to step in to avert events that pose unacceptable systemic risk" (Paulson 2008). The good news is that the markets will take this implicit guarantee seriously, particularly after the recent government guarantees offered in the course of taking over Fannie Mae and Freddie Mac,

Dwight M. Jaffee is the Willis Booth Professor of Finance and Real Estate at the Haas School of Business, University of California, Berkeley. Mark Perlow is a partner at K&L Gates LLP, focusing on investment management and securities law. Starting in 1994, he served in various roles at the Securities and Exchange Commission (SEC), including senior counsel in the Office of the SEC General Counsel from 1998 to 1999. This chapter was originally published in 2008.

but that is also the bad news. If investment banks believe they will be bailed out by the Fed, and if investment bankers do not believe that big losses will cost them their jobs, then they will have incentive to gamble with the taxpayers' money. In other words, future crises are to be expected, absent a regulatory solution.

We have no doubt that the Fed will be better prepared to deal with the next crisis, but remarkably neither the Fed, nor the Treasury, nor the SEC has offered any proposals to re-regulate the investment banks to minimize the *likelihood* of a future crisis. To fill this gap, we propose a regulatory mechanism modeled on the banking regulations that already protect our payment system. Our system will (1) minimize the need for a Fed bailout in a future investment bank crisis, (2) effectively maximize the role of market discipline in controlling investment bank risk management, and (3) maintain the overall efficiency of the U.S. capital markets. First, we must be clear on the conditions that led to the Fed's bailout of Bear Stearns, since an accurate understanding of these conditions is essential to creating a new regulatory framework that would render future interventions highly unlikely.

WHY THE FED HAD TO BAIL OUT BEAR STEARNS

An investment bank's activities can be divided into (among other parts) two key activities: (1) managing an investment portfolio, including stocks, bonds, and other instruments, and (2) operating as a central market maker and counterparty in the over-the-counter (OTC) derivatives market. Investment risks, if they become excessive, should be a concern for a bank's lenders and shareholders, but they do not pose a direct risk to the financial system unless investment losses prevent a bank from fulfilling its counterparty obligations in the derivatives market. Bear Stearns was rescued because it was "too interconnected to fail" due to its web of derivative contracts with the rest of the global financial system. These derivatives allow firms to speculate on or to hedge price risks arising from virtually all financial phenomena, especially from foreign exchange rate movements, interest rate fluctuations, and credit default events. They are mainly traded over the counter with an investment bank as the counterparty and are individually negotiated to be tailor-made in terms of principal amounts, maturity, payoff events, and other technical features (such as the strike price when the contract is an option). As a result of this large and sophisticated market, financial firms (including banks and hedge funds) have created a complex network of interlinking derivative positions—for example, hedge fund A enters into a swap with hedge fund B because it knows B has hedged certain risks with investment bank C. This network creates systemic risk as an externality, since if one key counterparty were to fail on its derivative obligations, the failure would likely create a cascade of failures larger than any single counterparty has the incentive to try to prevent.

The dollar amounts at issue are enormous. The Bank for International Settlements estimates that close to $600 trillion (that's right, trillion) in notional value of derivatives was outstanding at year-end 2007. To be sure, the notional value far exceeds the net economic value, in the same way that a prepaid one-year homeowner's policy on a $500,000 home (the notional amount) might have a market value of $1,500. Nevertheless, the net amounts and the number of contracts are still enormous, and should one dealer fail, counterparties would refuse to do business with each other because each could not understand whether the others were solvent. The financial system would freeze up long before the dealers or authorities could sort out the network.

POTENTIAL REFORMS

An immediate measure (one raised by Bernanke and Paulson and currently being explored by the major dealers) is to organize a clearinghouse for settling derivative positions. One possible clearinghouse arrangement is to make the derivatives exchange-traded, on an exchange such as the Chicago Mercantile Exchange. On such exchanges, the trade price is determined by the two traders, but the exchange itself becomes the counterparty for both traders. A second form of clearinghouse is to allow the dealers to net their obligations to each other, illustrated by the check-clearing mechanism in major financial centers. The major banks in New York City, for example, have daily claims in trillions of dollars on each other, but the clearinghouse allows them to clear the net amounts efficiently at the end of each business day. Both exchanges and check clearinghouses solve the problem that a participant could default on its obligations by creating a mutualized entity through which the participating brokers or banks agree to share in any possible losses. This mutualization also creates a form of market discipline, since each of the participants has a clear incentive to police its partners.

The problem with both of these measures is that they require only a limited number of standardized contracts to be traded. As on exchanges, there would have to be only a limited number of reference events or firms, notional amounts, maturity dates, strike prices, and the like. In contrast, the strength of the current OTC system arises precisely because traders highly value the ability to tailor an endless variety of derivatives to match their precise needs. Thus squeezing OTC derivatives onto a clearinghouse or an exchange would eliminate the very diversity that has made the market so important and useful.

This leaves us with the initial problem, namely, that, for better or for worse, the Fed has effectively guaranteed the liabilities of the largest investment banks, in particular their books of impaired and illiquid structured financial investments such as mortgage-backed securities and collateralized debt obligations, thus creating moral hazard for these banks to engage in excessively risky transactions. The result is that the normally constructive role of market discipline has weakened, because bank creditors now anticipate that the Fed will step in to rescue them. In other words, without further regulatory responses, the next crisis will likely be soon in coming and quite possibly even greater in magnitude. With this definition of the problem, we turn to our proposed solution.

REGULATORY RESPONSES

The Fed's unprecedented actions to avoid a Bear Stearns bankruptcy provide a prima facie case that the regulation of investment banks must be expanded. Bernanke and Paulson agree that any new regulation must be integrated with strong market discipline. However, for market discipline to be effective, investment banks must be allowed to fail. It will be difficult, if not impossible, for the Fed and the Treasury to square these two goals under the current regulatory regime. Indeed, market discipline during the Bear Stearns crisis took the destabilizing and destructive form of a bank run. The markets will not believe that the Fed will allow market discipline to run its course until it allows a major bank to fail; however, a Fed threat to do so is not credible as long as the investment banks remain too interconnected to fail. Thus regulation must be reformed to eliminate the link through which losses on an investment bank's investment portfolio threaten its ability to meet its obligations as a central counterparty in derivatives.

Our proposal is to improve investment bank regulation by separating the firms' investment activities from their derivatives counterparty activities. This separation would recognize that the counterparty system now parallels the payments system as a fundamental component of the financial system's infrastructure. The payments system and OTC derivatives system both create a network of interconnected positions and the resulting vulnerability that the failure of a large and central participant could create a cascade of failures and thereby a systemic failure. The regulatory structure that has successfully protected the U.S. payments system thus offers a template for protecting the counterparty network from risky investment activities. Current federal commercial banking law provides for a well-defined hierarchy of entities, for example:

- U.S. *commercial banks* may only carry out a "banking business"— primarily issuing deposits and making loans.
- U.S. *bank holding companies* may carry out activities "closely related to banking," as designated by the Fed. These permitted activities include the ownership of one or more commercial banks. A bank holding company that meets the Fed's highest risk-based capital rating—"well capitalized"—may also be certified as a "financial holding company."
- U.S. *financial holding companies* may carry out an even wider range of financial activities, most importantly investment banking and insurance.

This hierarchy structure operates, however, under the clear understanding that the holding companies operate to protect their commercial banks, and not the other way around. For example, special conditions of profitability and capital adequacy must be met before capital can be transferred "upstream" from a commercial bank to its holding company. This regulatory system has performed well since it was initiated almost ten years ago.

Our proposal is to create a comparable separation of an investment bank's counterparty operations from the risks and possible losses in its various investment activities. As mentioned earlier, U.S. investment banks currently operate (among others) two separate business lines: (1) running hedge fund-like trading operations that maintain a highly leveraged and maturity-mismatched portfolio of risky investments, and (2) operating as market makers and primary counterparties in the OTC market for financial derivatives. Absent separation of the two activities, market discipline will not eliminate the incentive of an investment bank to use the Fed's liquidity backstop as a means to take excessive risks in its trading operations.

Separating the risk-taking trading from the derivative counterparty operations thus seems to be the only way to implement Secretary Paulson's prescription that market discipline play a role in future investment bank regulation. The counterparty subsidiary would be closely supervised and regulated to ensure it could operate safely and dependably on a stand-alone basis. The trading operations, in contrast, would continue to have limited regulation, but any losses would fall entirely on the debt and equity owners of the investment bank. These investors would thus have every incentive to enforce market discipline on the investment bank's risk management activities. The Fed's only action with a failing investment bank would be to spin off the counterparty division to a stand-alone firm or to merge it with another sound derivative dealer.

If our regulatory system had been in place two years ago, the Bear Stearns bailout could have been avoided, for two reasons. First, with a recognition that regulators would have no need to bail out an investment bank suffering even severe investment losses, lenders would have been more reluctant to provide funding for the highly leveraged, maturity-mismatched, and fundamentally risky Bear Stearns investment portfolio. In other words, market discipline would have acted to force Bear Stearns to limit the investment strategy that was the source of the losses that precipitated the firm's failure. Second, even if Bear Stearns had succeeded in obtaining funding for its risky investment portfolio, the Federal Reserve would have had no reason to bail out the firm, since the counterparty network of derivatives would have continued to function normally while the Bear Stearns investment portfolio was being liquidated by the firm's creditors.

IN BRIEF

Our proposal is to apply the principles of the existing commercial bank holding company laws to separate investment bank counterparty obligations from their investment portfolio risks. This would require new legislation to parallel the existing Gramm-Leach-Bliley Act of 1999, which relaxed Glass-Steagall by allowing a well-capitalized commercial bank to own an investment bank. Under our proposal, an investment bank could continue to carry out both trading and derivative counterparty activities, but new legislation would safeguard all derivative counterparty obligations from losses that might arise from risky investment bank trading portfolios. In this manner, regulation and market discipline would combine to protect the financial system's infrastructure, without creating unnecessary regulatory burdens.

REFERENCES AND FURTHER READING

Bernanke, Ben. 2008. "Reducing Systemic Risk." Speech given at Jackson Hole, Wyoming, August 22. Available at www.federalreserve.gov /newsevents/speech/bernanke20080822a.htm.

Cox, Christopher. 2008. "Testimony Concerning Recent Events in the Credit Markets." Testimony before the U.S. Senate Committee on Banking, Housing and Urban Affairs, April 3. Available at www.sec .gov/news/testimony/2008/ts040308cc.htm.

Geithner, Timothy. 2008. "Actions by the New York Fed in Response to Liquidity Pressures in Financial Markets." Testimony before the U.S. Senate Committee on Banking, Housing and Urban Affairs, April 3. Available at www.newyorkfed.org/newsevents/speeches/2008 /gei080403.html.

Paulson, Henry. 2008. "Remarks on the Markets and the Economy." Speech given at the Exchequer Club, July 31. Available at www.ustreas .gov/press/releases/hp1107.htm.

CHAPTER 17

Why Paulson Is Wrong

Luigi Zingales

WHEN A PROFITABLE company is hit by a very large liability, as was the case in 1985 when Texaco lost a $12 billion court case against Pennzoil, the solution is not to have the government buy its assets at inflated prices: the solution is Chapter 11. In Chapter 11, companies with a solid underlying business generally swap debt for equity: the old equity holders are wiped out, and the old debt claims are transformed into equity claims in the new entity, which continues operating with a new capital structure. Alternatively, the debt holders can agree to cut down the face value of debt in exchange for some warrants. Even before Chapter 11, these procedures were the solutions adopted to deal with the large railroad bankruptcies at the turn of the twentieth century. So why not use this well-established approach to solve the financial sector's current problems?

Luigi Zingales is the Robert C. McCormack Professor of Entrepreneurship and Finance, University of Chicago Graduate School of Business, has won the 2003 Bernacer Prize for the best European young financial economist and the 2002 NASDAQ award for best paper in capital formation, and is the author, together with Raghuram G. Rajan, of *Saving Capitalism from the Capitalists*. This chapter was originally published in 2008.

The obvious answer is that we do not have time; Chapter 11 procedures are generally long and complex, and the crisis has reached a point where time is of the essence. If left to the negotiations of the parties involved, this process will take months, and we do not have this luxury. However, we are in extraordinary times, and the government has taken, and is prepared to take, unprecedented measures. As if rescuing the American International Group (AIG) and prohibiting all short-selling of financial stocks was not enough, now Treasury Secretary Paulson proposes a sort of Resolution Trust Corporation (RTC) that will buy out (with taxpayers' money) the distressed assets of the financial sector. But at what price?

If banks and financial institutions find it difficult to recapitalize (i.e., issue new equity), it is because the private sector is uncertain about the value of the assets they have in their portfolio and does not want to overpay. Would the government be better in valuing those assets? No. In a negotiation between a government official and banker with a bonus at risk, who will have more clout in determining the price? The Paulson RTC will buy toxic assets at inflated prices, thereby creating a charitable institution that provides welfare to the rich—at the taxpayers' expense.

If the RTC subsidy is large enough, it will succeed in stopping the crisis. But, again, at what price? The answer: billions of dollars in taxpayer money and, even worse, the violation of the fundamental capitalist principle that she who reaps the gains also bears the losses. Remember that in the Savings and Loan crisis, the government *had* to bail out those institutions because the deposits were federally insured. But in this case the government *does not have* to bail out the debt holders of Bear Sterns, AIG, or any of the other financial institutions that will benefit from the Paulson RTC.

Since we do not have time for a Chapter 11 and we do not want to bail out all the creditors, the lesser evil is to do what judges do in contentious and overextended bankruptcy processes: to cram down a restructuring plan on creditors, where part of the debt is forgiven in exchange for some equity or some warrants.

There is precedent for such a bold move. During the Great Depression, many debt contracts were indexed to gold. So when the dollar convertibility into gold was suspended, the value of that debt soared, threatening the survival of many institutions. The Roosevelt administration declared the clause invalid, de facto forcing debt forgiveness. The Supreme Court upheld this decision.

My colleague and current Fed Governor Randall Kroszner studied this episode and showed that not only stock prices, but bond prices as well, soared after the Supreme Court upheld the decision. How is that possible? As corporate finance experts have been saying for the last thirty years, there are real costs from having too much debt and too little equity in the capital structure, and a reduction in the face value of debt can sometimes benefit not only the equity holders but also the debt holders.

If debt forgiveness benefits both equity and debt holders, why do debt holders not voluntarily agree to it? First, there is a coordination problem. Even if each individual debt holder benefits from a reduction in the face value of debt, she will benefit even more if everybody else cuts the face value of their debt and she does not. Hence, everybody waits for the other to move first, creating obvious delay. Second, from a debt holder point of view, a government bailout is better. Even talk of a government bailout reduces the debt holders' incentives to act, making the government bailout more necessary.

As during the Great Depression, and in many debt restructurings, it makes sense in the current contingency to mandate a partial debt forgiveness or a debt-for-equity swap in the financial sector. It has the benefit of being a well-tested strategy in the private sector, and it leaves the taxpayers out of the picture. But if it is so simple, why has no expert mentioned it?

The major players in the financial sector do not like it. It is much more appealing for the financial industry to be bailed out at the taxpayers' expense than to bear their share of pain. Forcing a debt-for-equity swap or a debt forgiveness would be no greater a violation of private property rights than a massive bailout, but it faces much stronger political opposition.

The appeal of the Paulson solution is that it taxes the many and benefits the few. Since the many (we, the taxpayers) are dispersed, we cannot put up a good fight on Capitol Hill, while the financial industry is well represented at all the levels. For six of the last thirteen years, the Secretary of Treasury was a Goldman Sachs alumnus. But financial experts are also responsible for this silence. Just as it is difficult to find a doctor willing to testify against another doctor in a malpractice suit, no matter how egregious the case, finance experts in both political parties are too friendly to the industry in which they study and work.

The decisions that Congress must make now will matter not just to the prospects of the U.S. economy in the year to come, but they will shape the type of capitalism we will live in for the next fifty years. Do we want to live in a system where profits are private, but losses are socialized? Where taxpayer money is used to prop up failed firms? Or do we want to live in a system where people are held responsible for their decisions, where imprudent behavior is penalized and prudent behavior rewarded?

For somebody like me, who believes strongly in the free market system, the most serious risk of the current situation is that the interest of a few financiers will undermine the fundamental workings of the capitalist system. The time has come to save capitalism from the capitalists.

CHAPTER 18

Dr. StrangeLoan: Or, How I Learned to Stop Worrying and Love the Financial Collapse

Aaron S. Edlin

THE WORLD ALMOST changed Wednesday, September 17, 2008.

For years, the U.S. government debt soared. For years, the U.S. Treasury borrowed more and more funds. For years the government paid obscene sums in interest to service the debt. All that almost came to an end on Wednesday, September 17, 2008. That day, a light shone at the end of the tunnel, and the government almost found a way out of this "business" of borrowing money and entered the business of guarding money, an honorable and profitable business that Brink's

Aaron S. Edlin holds the Richard W. Jennings Endowed Chair and is Professor of Economics and of Law at the University of California, Berkeley, and a Research Associate at the National Bureau of Economic Research. He is co-author with P. Areeda and L. Kaplow of a leading antitrust casebook. He was formerly the senior economist covering regulation, antitrust, and industrial organization at the President's Council of Economic Advisers, and has taught or held research positions at Yale, Stanford, and Columbia.

security company and vault makers like Diebold have enjoyed for years.

On September 17, the interest rate on ninety-day Treasuries fell to three basis points. That is 75 cents of interest on $10,000 of borrowing. Government borrowing was essentially free. And the interest rate, falling fast, seemed sure to go negative. Surely Treasury rates would have gone negative had the Bush administration not come out Thursday with its new plan to buy up toxic financial paper.

Think how close we were to finding a solution to the problems of debt and taxes. The government could earn money simply by offering to guard funds!

COMING TO GRIPS WITH NEGATIVE INTEREST RATES

What would negative interest on Treasuries mean? No more costs from servicing the debt. People would be paying the Treasury for the privilege of using their money. Sound strange?

Well, in real terms, after deducting inflation, the Treasury has been paying substantially negative interest for a while, at least on shorter term borrowing. But the Treasury was still paying positive nominal interest, so a T-bill was substantially better than holding cash or keeping funds in a non-interest-bearing account.

Why, you ask, would anyone pay another in nominal terms to use their cash instead of the reverse? Wouldn't it be better to just keep the cash at home stuffed in a mattress?

The simple fact is that you could easily lose all the money in your mattress from theft or in a fire. People have been paying Brinks or vault makers for years to secure cash against thieves. So, now we were simply on the verge of paying the U.S. Treasury to do the same thing—safeguard our cash.

You just have to change your mind-set from paying someone to use your money to paying someone to guard your money. Guarding your money is a service for which it is eminently sensible to pay.

THE TREASURY'S VALUE PROPOSITION

Every business must have a value proposition: the more unique the better.

For years, the U.S. Treasury has issued bonds borrowing money in competition with America's leading firms or other government borrowers. Typically, the U.S. Treasury offered investors lower returns but promised more safety—safety (or "quality") was always the Treasury's niche.

On Wednesday, September 17, 2008, no longer did money market funds, banks, or anyone else offer the U.S. Treasury any serious competition. So safe did Treasuries look by comparison that the Treasury could pay nothing for your money and people gladly handed it over. And it seemed likely that by Thursday, the Treasury would enter a whole new world in which interest rates were negative and we paid the Treasury for safeguarding our funds.

How would the Treasury compete with other purveyors of security services? Bepress, like all firms, must meet payroll and other costs, so I wondered where to store the money needed to do so. The money currently sat perilously in a money market deposit account at a bank. Treasuries were at zero and possibly heading negative. Could keeping our notional accounting "cash" in the form of real cash be the best option? A few calls to security companies made it clear that guarding a big pile of greenbacks for ninety days would be very expensive. Interest rates on Treasuries would need to go very negative before the U.S. Treasury found any serious competition from security companies.

What a value proposition the Treasury stumbled on!

COULD THE TREASURY SOLVE THE GOVERNMENT'S
DEBT PROBLEM?

It seemed that the Bush administration had found a perfect solution to the government's financial problems. Instead of paying tons of money to service the massive debt the government had accumulated, now that all of Wall Street seemed on the verge of collapse, now that Paul Volker and Laurence Lindsey were warning us that the payment system (i.e., banks) could be next, the U.S. Treasury was in an incomparable competitive position. On one side of the market, it had other borrowers who had no credibility of repayment and could not compete, and on the other it had security companies who require significant sums to guard your cash behind guns, steel, and cement, and could not compete. With this kind of market power, the Treasury could have profited enormously by charging negative interest rates, eliminated our government debt problem before too long, and then begun cutting taxes to the quick.

Sadly, the Bush administration did not realize how close they were to solving the government's troubles, and instead, I fear they stepped into some more. On Thursday, the Bush administration came up with a plan to bail out the private financial system, destroying the Treasury's competitive advantage by shoring up the Treasury's competitive rivals in borrowing. Not only does the government now bear the costs of other borrowers failing to repay, but it must now again pay significant sums for its own borrowing. In the best of all worlds, if this works out very well, then at substantial cost to the taxpayer, we will be back where we started. The government will be paying huge sums to service its even larger debt. And the Wall Street bankers will be back in business raking it in.

FURTHER READING

U.S. Treasury. 2008. "Daily Treasury Yield Curve Rates." Available at www.ustreas.gov/offices/domestic-finance/debt-management /interest-rate/yield.shtml.

CHAPTER 19

Questioning the Treasury's $700 Billion Blank Check: An Open Letter to Secretary Paulson

Aaron S. Edlin

DEAR SECRETARY PAULSON,

Today, I read the U.S. Treasury's humble request for the authority to spend 700 billion taxpayer-owned dollars. This taxpayer's answer: "No."

Sorry, Mr. Paulson, for the vote of no confidence, but consider the terms you propose. The only hard restriction on this gift certificate is that it must be redeemed at "a financial institution having its headquarters in the United States" and used to buy "mortgage-related

Aaron S. Edlin holds the Richard W. Jennings Endowed Chair and is Professor of Economics and of Law at the University of California, Berkeley, and a Research Associate at the National Bureau of Economic Research. He is co-author with Phillip Areeda and Lewis Kaplow of a leading antitrust casebook. He was formerly the senior economist covering regulation, antitrust, and industrial organization at the President's Council of Economic Advisers, and he has taught or held research positions at Yale, Stanford, and Columbia.

assets." You will have little trouble spending this bounty, probably all before Election Day.

I did notice the soft restriction, with the two "Considerations" that you are intended to "consider" in your purchases: "(1) providing stability or preventing disruption to the financial markets or banking system; and (2) protecting the taxpayer."

It is kind of you to remember the taxpayer, but will you forgive me for being a little concerned when your proposed legislation provides no clue how you are to balance these two considerations nor what constitutes adequate protection of the taxpayer?

Just as I am wondering whether you are allowed by chance to pay inflated prices for assets if you should so choose and if you judge it to promote "stability," I come upon the fact that your decisions will be "non-reviewable and committed to agency discretion, and may not be reviewed by any court of law or any administrative agency."

I stopped dead on reading this. You, the Treasury Secretary, are really asking for a $700 billion blank check.

The legislation does not even suggest that you should try to get a fair price, not, anyway, if "stability" is at stake. And if you decide to give twice the fair price to an old friend from your Goldman Sachs days and think this contributes to stability, that decision is non-reviewable. What a job you have! To think that only last week I felt sorry for you.

You could, under this legislation, pay $700 billion for "paper" having a face value of $800 billion, even though the paper's market value has sunk to $100 billion or even though the paper has no market, so long as you think the purchase promotes stability sufficiently. You could do so with no review and no appeal. I suppose, taking the words of your legislation literally, you could spend the entire $700 billion buying a single mortgage owned by Goldman Sachs if you thought such a cash injection was just the trick.

To be sure, you might be successfully challenged in court on the more ludicrous hypothetical purchase, despite the no-judicial review clause. On the other hand, I can well imagine Justice Scalia's opinion scolding Congress for not drafting better and telling the plaintiff to pound sand.

Regardless of such far-fetched possibilities it is clear that the proposed legislation gives you nearly complete authority to make bad deals in the name of stability—bad deals for taxpayers and good for your brethren on Wall Street.

And here is a disturbing thought: If the initial tab is $700 billion, is it possible you may wind up coming back for much more? Could the administration that brought us the $2 trillion war bring us a $2 trillion bailout?

Finally, would it be over-the-top cynical to worry that after you give some investment bank a particularly sweet deal that the bank or its employees would later decide to spend some of that money in campaign contributions or political action committees?

I dearly hope this legislation is not passed as it stands. If anything like this bailout must be done, I propose putting Warren Buffett, and not Henry Paulson, in charge. Warren Buffett and Charlie Munger have a strong history of getting assets at a discount when sellers need liquidity. The goal should be stated in the legislation: buy assets at a bargain in cases where the purchase will improve the stability of the financial markets or the banking system. The alternative to selling should be a quick trip to a special panel of bankruptcy judges ready to impose a debt for equity swap, as proposed by Luigi Zingales.

The government made a profit on the Chrysler bailout, and I see no reason why that shouldn't happen here. No reason, that is, except the proposed legislation.

Appendix: Treasury Department Proposed Legislation

The following is the legislative proposal from the Treasury Department for authority to buy mortgage-related assets:

Sec. 1. Short Title.

This Act may be cited as _____.

Sec. 2. Purchases of Mortgage-Related Assets.

(a) Authority to Purchase.—The Secretary is authorized to purchase, and to make and fund commitments to purchase, on such terms and conditions as determined by the Secretary, mortgage-related assets from any financial institution having its headquarters in the United States.

(b) Necessary Actions.—The Secretary is authorized to take such actions as the Secretary deems necessary to carry out the authorities in this Act, including, without limitation:

(1) appointing such employees as may be required to carry out the authorities in this Act and defining their duties;

(2) entering into contracts, including contracts for services authorized by section 3109 of title 5, United States Code, without regard to any other provision of law regarding public contracts;

(3) designating financial institutions as financial agents of the Government, and they shall perform all such reasonable duties related to this Act as financial agents of the Government as may be required of them;

(4) establishing vehicles that are authorized, subject to supervision by the Secretary, to purchase mortgage-related assets and issue obligations; and

(5) issuing such regulations and other guidance as may be necessary or appropriate to define terms or carry out the authorities of this Act.

Sec. 3. Considerations.

In exercising the authorities granted in this Act, the Secretary shall take into consideration means for—

(1) providing stability or preventing disruption to the financial markets or banking system; and

(2) protecting the taxpayer.

Sec. 4. Reports to Congress.

Within three months of the first exercise of the authority granted in section 2(a), and semiannually thereafter, the Secretary shall report to the Committees on the Budget, Financial Services, and Ways and

Means of the House of Representatives and the Committees on the Budget, Finance, and Banking, Housing, and Urban Affairs of the Senate with respect to the authorities exercised under this Act and the considerations required by section 3.

Sec. 5. Rights; Management; Sale of Mortgage-Related Assets.

(a) Exercise of Rights.—The Secretary may, at any time, exercise any rights received in connection with mortgage-related assets purchased under this Act.

(b) Management of Mortgage-Related Assets.—The Secretary shall have authority to manage mortgage-related assets purchased under this Act, including revenues and portfolio risks therefrom.

(c) Sale of Mortgage-Related Assets.—The Secretary may, at any time, upon terms and conditions and at prices determined by the Secretary, sell, or enter into securities loans, repurchase transactions, or other financial transactions in regard to, any mortgage-related asset purchased under this Act.

(d) Application of Sunset to Mortgage-Related Assets.—The authority of the Secretary to hold any mortgage-related asset purchased under this Act before the termination date in section 9, or to purchase or fund the purchase of a mortgage-related asset under a commitment entered into before the termination date in section 9, is not subject to the provisions of section 9.

Sec. 6. Maximum Amount of Authorized Purchases.

The Secretary's authority to purchase mortgage-related assets under this Act shall be limited to $700,000,000,000 outstanding at any one time

Sec. 7. Funding.

For the purpose of the authorities granted in this Act, and for the costs of administering those authorities, the Secretary may use the proceeds of the sale of any securities issued under chapter 31 of title 31, United States Code, and the purposes for which securities may be issued under chapter 31 of title 31, United States Code, are extended to include actions authorized by this Act, including the payment of administrative expenses. Any funds expended for actions authorized by this Act, including the payment of administrative expenses, shall be deemed appropriated at the time of such expenditure.

Sec. 8. Review.

Decisions by the Secretary pursuant to the authority of this Act are non-reviewable and committed to agency discretion, and may not be reviewed by any court of law or any administrative agency.

Sec. 9. Termination of Authority.

The authorities under this Act, with the exception of authorities granted in sections 2(b)(5), 5, and 7, shall terminate two years from the date of enactment of this Act.

Sec. 10. Increase in Statutory Limit on the Public Debt.

Subsection (b) of section 3101 of title 31, United States Code, is amended by striking out the dollar limitation contained in such subsection and inserting in lieu thereof $11,315,000,000,000.

Sec. 11. Credit Reform.

The costs of purchases of mortgage-related assets made under section 2(a) of this Act shall be determined as provided under the Federal Credit Reform Act of 1990, as applicable.

Sec. 12. Definitions.

For purposes of this section, the following definitions shall apply:

(1) Mortgage-Related Assets.—The term "mortgage-related assets" means residential or commercial mortgages and any securities, obligations, or other instruments that are based on or related to such mortgages, that in each case was originated or issued on or before September 17, 2008.

(2) Secretary.—The term "Secretary" means the Secretary of the Treasury.

(3) United States.—The term "United States" means the States, territories, and possessions of the United States and the District of Columbia.

REFERENCES AND FURTHER READING

Stiglitz, Joseph. 2006. "The High Cost of the Iraq War." *The Economists' Voice* 3, no. 3: art. 5. Available at www.bepress.com/ev/vol3/iss3/art5.

U.S. Treasury Department. 2008. Proposed legislation. Available at www .bepress.com/cgi/viewcontent.cgi?context=ev&article=1408&file name=0&type=additional.

Zingales, Luigi. 2008. "Why Paulson Is Wrong." *The Economists' Voice* 5, no. 5: art. 2. Available at www.bepress.com/ev/vol5/iss5/art2.

CHAPTER 20

Auction Design Critical for Rescue Plan

Lawrence M. Ausubel and Peter Cramton

THE TREASURY PROPOSES to invest $700 billion in mortgage-related securities to resolve the financial crisis, using market mechanisms such as reverse auctions to determine prices. A well-designed auction process can indeed be an effective tool for acquiring distressed assets at minimum cost to the taxpayer. However, a simplistic process could lead to higher cost and fewer securities purchased. It is critical for the auction process to be designed carefully.

The immediate crisis is one of illiquidity. Banks hold a variety of mortgage-backed securities, some almost worthless, while others retain considerable value. None can be sold, except at fire-sale prices. The Treasury proposes to restore liquidity by stepping in and purchasing these securities. But at what price?

Lawrence M. Ausubel and Peter Cramton are Professors of Economics at the University of Maryland and experts in the theory and practice of auction design.

A SIMPLE APPROACH LEADS TO OVERPAYMENT

A simple but naïve approach would be to invite the holders of all mortgage-related securities to bid in a single reverse auction. The Treasury sets an overall quantity of securities to be purchased. The auctioneer starts at a price of nearly 100 cents on the dollar. All holders of illiquid securities would presumably be happy to sell at nearly face value, so there would be excess supply. The auctioneer then progressively lowers the price—90 cents, 80 cents, and so on—and bidders indicate the securities that they are willing to sell at each lower price. Eventually, a price, perhaps 30 cents, is reached at which supply equals demand. The Treasury buys the securities offered at the clearing pricing, paying 30 cents on the dollar.

This simplistic approach is fatally flawed. The Treasury pays 30 cents on the dollar, purchasing all mortgage-related securities worth less than 30 cents on the dollar. Perhaps, on average, the purchased securities are worth 15 cents on the dollar. The Treasury buys only the worst of the worst, intervening in a way that rewards the least deserving. And, as a result of overpaying drastically, the Treasury can mop up relatively few distressed securities with its limited budget.

In the simplistic approach, competition among different securities overshadows competition within securities and among bidders. The auction merely identifies which securities are least valuable rather than determining the securities' value. An auction that determines a real price for a given security needs to require multiple holders of the security to compete with one another. This can be achieved if the Treasury purchases only some, not all, of any given security.

A BETTER APPROACH

Thus a better approach would be for the Treasury to instead conduct a separate auction for each security and limit itself to buying perhaps 50 percent of the aggregate face value. Again, the auction starts at a high price and works its way down. If the security clears at 30 cents on the dollar, this means that the holders value it at 30 cents on the dollar. (If the value were only 15 cents, then most holders would supply 100 percent of their securities to be purchased at 30 cents, and the price would be pushed lower.) The auction then works as intended. The price is reasonably close to value. The "winners" are the bidders who value the asset the least and value liquidity the most.

This auction has an important additional benefit. The "losers" are not left high and dry. By determining the market clearing price, the auction increases liquidity for the remaining 50 percent of face value, as well as for related securities. The auction has effectively aggregated market information about the security's value. This price information is the essential ingredient needed to restore the secondary market for mortgage-backed securities.

Handling many securities is a straightforward extension. Different but related securities can be grouped together in the same auction and purchased simultaneously. Each security has its own price. The bidders indicate the quantity of each security they would like to sell at the specified prices. The price is reduced for any security with excess supply, and the process repeats until a clearing price is found for each security.

Auctioning many related securities simultaneously gives the bidders some flexibility to adjust positions as the market gradually clears. This improves price formation and enables bidders to better manage their liquidity needs. As a result, efficiency improves and taxpayer costs are further reduced.

For this auction design to work well, there needs to be sufficient competition. This should not be a problem for securities with diffuse ownership. For securities with more concentrated ownership, various approaches are possible. The Treasury could buy a smaller percentage of the face value. Alternatively, the Treasury could purchase the securities with the explicit understanding that the securities would be sold by auction some months or years in the future, after the liquidity crisis is over. To the extent that the securities are sold at a lower price, the holder would contractually owe the Treasury the difference, plus interest.

One sensible approach for the sequencing of auctions is to start with the best of the worst; that is, begin the auctioning with a group of securities that are among the least toxic. These will be easier for bidders to assess, and the auction can proceed more quickly. Then, subsequent auctions can move on to the increasingly problematic securities. In this way, the information revealed in the earlier auctions will facilitate the later auctions.

The basic auction approach suggested here is neither new nor untested. It was introduced over the last ten years and has been used successfully in many countries to auction tens of billions of dollars in electricity and gas contracts. It is quite similar to the approach that has been used to auction more than $100 billion in the mobile telephone spectrum worldwide. It is a dynamic version of the approach that financial markets use for share repurchases. If implemented correctly, each auction can be completed in less than one day.

Thus the auction approach meets the three main requirements of the rescue plan: (1) to provide a quick and effective means for the Treasury to purchase mortgage-related assets and increase liquidity; (2) to yield prices that are closely related to value; and (3) to provide a transparent, rules-based mechanism that treats different security holders consistently and leaves minimal scope for discretion or favoritism.

Indeed, the second and third requirements may be decisive for obtaining broad political support. The main alternative to auctions put forward by the Treasury is to employ professional asset managers. To the extent that negotiations or other individualized trading arrangements are used, the public will be rightfully wary that favoritism may be exerted and that some security holders will be offered sweetheart deals. By contrast, a transparent auction process is readily subjected to oversight.

The Treasury appears to be embarking on the greatest public intervention into financial markets since the Great Depression. The ultimate success or failure of the intervention may depend on the fine details of the auction design. Let's get it right.

CHAPTER 21

A Better Plan for Addressing the Financial Crisis

Lucian A. Bebchuk

THE CURRENT FINANCIAL crisis is widely viewed as the most serious since the Great Depression. Last week, facing severe market reactions to the failures of American International Group (AIG) and Lehman Brothers, the U.S. Treasury Department put forward a bold and massive program of spending up to $700 billion on purchasing "troubled assets" from financial institutions.

This chapter critiques this proposed emergency legislation. It also puts forward a superior alternative for advancing the two goals of the proposed legislation—restoring stability to the financial markets and protecting taxpayers. I show that the proposed legislation can be redesigned to limit greatly the cost to taxpayers while performing better in terms of restoring stability to the financial markets.

Lucian A. Bebchuk is the William J. Friedman and Alicia Townsend Friedman Professor of Law, Economics, and Finance and Director of the Program on Corporate Governance at Harvard Law School. He is also a Research Associate of the National Bureau of Economic Research. This chapter develops some of the points made in an op-ed piece he published in *The Wall Street Journal*.

Although it is widely accepted that the current problems in the financial system result from problems in the housing market, the emergency legislation and my analysis in this chapter focus on the current crisis of liquidity, capitalization, and confidence in the financial sector. Throughout, I accept the two stated objectives of the Treasury's plan—restoring stability to the financial sector and protecting taxpayers—and show how they can be better served by a redesigned plan.

The proposed redesign is based on four interrelated elements:

- *No overpaying for troubled assets.* The Treasury's authority to purchase troubled assets should be limited to doing so at fair market value.
- *Addressing undercapitalization problems directly.* Because the purchase of troubled assets at fair market value may leave financial firms severely undercapitalized, the Treasury's authority should be expanded to allow purchasing, again at fair market value, new securities issued by financial institutions in need of additional capital.
- *Market-based discipline.* To ensure that purchases are made at fair market value, the Treasury should conduct them through multi-buyer competitive processes with appropriate incentives.
- *Inducing infusion of private capital.* To further expand the capital available to the financial sector, and to reduce the use of public funds for this purpose, financial firms should be required or induced to raise capital through right offerings to their existing shareholders.

Below I discuss in turn each of these four elements. In my analysis I discuss the major flaws of the proposed legislation that would undermine its effectiveness, and I explain how the plan I put forward can address them.

PURCHASING TROUBLED ASSETS

The premise of the Treasury's plan is that the current crisis is due to the presence of "toxic" real estate paper on the balance sheets. Financial firms can currently sell these "troubled assets" only at an extremely deep discount to face value, if at all. The Treasury believes that the presence of these illiquid troubled assets "clogs" the financial system and is "choking off the flow of credit." Because of the substantial presence of these illiquid troubled assets on the balance sheets of financial firms, the Treasury believes, financial firms have difficulty raising capital, are subject to risks of creditor runs, and are reluctant to carry out fully their role in financing the real economy.

One reason troubled assets cannot currently be sold at face value is probably due to the decline in the fundamental economic value of these assets due to the correction in the housing market. The Treasury believes, however, that financial firms cannot currently sell these assets even at their reduced fundamental value. In a normal, well-functioning market, with sufficient supply of interested buyers, such assets can be expected to trade at their fundamental value—the discounted present value of their "hold-to-maturity value." The Treasury believes, however, that we currently do not have such a normal, well-functioning market. Rather, we have a "limits to arbitrage" situation in which money managers that would otherwise be willing to purchase financial assets at any price below their fundamental value do not have sufficient liquidity to keep prices at fundamental values. The proposed legislation seeks to provide such liquidity through the use of public funds.

Accepting the need and desirability of using public funds to provide liquidity to the market for troubled assets, the critical issue concerns the price at which the Treasury would attempt to buy these assets. The Treasury's official statements about the plan contemplate purchasing troubled assets at fair value: "The price of assets purchased will be established through market mechanism where possible, such as reverse auctions." Such an approach is appealing, of course, because purchasing assets at fair market value might enable taxpayers to get an adequate return on their investment.

While the Treasury's statements contemplate purchases at fair market value, however, the draft legislation is careful to grant the Treasury full authority to pay higher prices for troubled assets. As Aaron Edlin and others have pointed out, the draft would permit the Treasury, if it so chooses, to spend, say, $700 billion for troubled assets with a fair value of only $200 billion, making taxpayers poorer by half a trillion dollars.

This freedom to confer massive gifts on private parties is highly problematic. It should be constrained: the legislation should direct the Treasury to buy assets at fair market value.

Some might ask whether directing the Treasury to purchase troubled assets only at fair market value might not make the purchase program inconsequential. Would this prescription not lead the Treasury to purchase troubled assets at fire-sale prices and thus not add significantly to the options available to firms? Accepting the diagnosis of our current predicament underlying the Treasury's proposal, the answer is no. At present, the prices are viewed as substantially below fundamental value due to the drying up of liquidity and the lack of fund supply that ensures pricing at fundamental value in normal times. Thus, the fair market value that the Treasury would pay would be one that would reflect market outcomes under conditions of adequate liquidity. What mechanism will best ensure that the prices paid for troubled assets purchased for taxpayers would indeed reflect such outcomes is a question I will take up later on.

DEALING DIRECTLY WITH UNDERCAPITALIZATION PROBLEMS

By itself, imposing the fair market value constraint on purchases of troubled assets might leave us with stability concerns that the Treasury sought to address by retaining the power to overpay. Because the depressed housing market reduced the fundamental value of troubled assets, some financial firms may well remain seriously undercapitalized even if they could sell troubled assets at fair value. The Treasury wants the power to overpay for troubled assets to be able to improve the capital position of these firms to restore stability and prevent creditor runs.

Let us suppose, for the time being, as the Treasury's plan does, that an infusion of additional capital to financial firms must at this point come, at least to a substantial degree, from the government. Even so, such an infusion of capital should not be done by giving gifts to the shareholders and bondholders of financial firms through overpaying for their assets. Rather, the provision of such additional capital should be done directly, aboveboard, and for consideration.

While the Treasury's draft legislation gives it large and unusual powers, some of which need to be scaled back, there is one power that the Treasury was not given but should be. The draft legislation allows the Treasury to purchase only preexisting assets. This limitation shoots taxpayers in the foot, preventing the government from getting newly issued securities from firms receiving capital infusions from it. This limitation should be revised to allow the Treasury to purchase—again only at fair market value—new securities in financial firms when doing so is necessary for stabilizing financial markets.

Authorizing the provision of capital in return for newly issued securities is far superior to authorizing, as the current draft does, the provision of capital through overpaying for troubled assets. To begin, taxpayers would be better protected; they would get adequate consideration for the capital they are providing rather than nothing at all, as under the Treasury's plan, which provides capital through subsidized purchases of troubled assets.

Furthermore, the direct approach would do a better job in providing capital where it is most useful. If the proposed legislation were implemented, capital would be inefficiently channeled, as the amount of troubled assets sold by firms would not necessarily be related to the amount of capital that they need and should get from the government.

Before moving on, I should comment on another approach that some lawmakers (such as Senator Christopher Dodd) and commentators (such as Paul Krugman) have raised: directing the government to insist on getting some newly issued securities—shares or warrants—in financial firms from which the government would purchase troubled assets. These proposals have been motivated by similar concerns to the one I have—that the Treasury's plan contemplates subsidizing some firm through overpaying for their troubled assets. To the extent that such overpaying will happen to shore up the firms' capital positions, these observers ask, why should the government not get at least some equity tickets to compensate it for the subsidized purchase of troubled assets?

While the motivation for these suggestions is understandable, and while they go in the direction I advocate—preventing the government from subsidizing firms from which troubled assets are purchased—they still unnecessarily tie together purchases of troubled assets and provision of new capital. Such a tie-in does not reduce the government's need for information or make matters otherwise simpler: the government would still need to assess how much it is overpaying for the purchased troubled assets and what new equity tickets would provide adequate consideration for the amount overpaid, which would require the government to determine both the fair market value of the troubled assets and the fair market value of new equity securities issued to it.

In such a case there would be no reason not to proceed in a manner reflecting explicitly and aboveboard the transactions taking place—that is, specify separately the price paid for the troubled assets (in a transaction aimed at paying fair market value for them) and the price paid for the new equity securities (in a transaction aimed at paying fair market value for them). Moreover, tying equity participations to purchases of troubled assets is problematic because of the already mentioned lack of correlation between the need for governmental purchases of troubled assets and the desirability of governmental infusion of capital. Some financial firms would like to sell a substantial amount of troubled assets to the government but do not need a governmental infusion of capital; and, conversely, some financial firms would need a capital infusion but would not wish to make significant use of the government's willingness to purchase troubled assets.

Before concluding the discussion of capital provision for adequate consideration in newly issued securities, it should be stressed that this is possible only for financial firms that are undercapitalized but still solvent. If a firm is insolvent and its shares thus do not have a positive fundamental value, any number of new equity securities may be insufficient to provide the government with adequate consideration. In such a case the process of infusing new capital for adequate consideration—whose implementation I describe below—would not result in an infusion of new capital. Even in a highly liquid and well-functioning market, a firm that is insolvent would not be able to get capital by selling additional equity participations.

Thus, even with (1) a mechanism for using public funds to provide liquidity to the market for troubled assets and to enable firms to sell such assets at fair value, and (2) a mechanism for using public funds to provide liquidity to the market for new capital for financial firms to enable such firms to sell new equity shares at fair market value, the government might well face a subset of financial firms that would be insolvent. For those firms that are either federally insured (banks) or whose bankruptcy would have sufficiently large negative system-wide effects, the government may decide to have a "bailout." Such a bailout, however, should involve wiping out shareholders' stakes, with the government effectively getting the full value of equity in return for its support. For those firms that are not federally insured and whose bankruptcy would not be judged to have sufficiently large, negative, system-wide effects, the government should let the insolvency proceed through standard processes (as it has decided to do in the case of Lehman Brothers).

Because the decline in the fundamental value of troubled assets may have rendered some financial firms truly insolvent, some bailouts and/or bankruptcies of financial firms may be unavoidable even under the proposed plan for using public funds to purchase troubled assets and new equity securities at fair value. However, that would hardly mean that the availability of the above-mentioned mechanisms (1) and (2)—using public funds to provide liquidity in the markets for troubled assets and new capital for financial firms—would not be valuable. These mechanisms would ensure that bailouts and bankruptcies would be limited to that subset of firms—which would hopefully turn out not to be substantial in scope—that would be insolvent even in the absence of liquidity problems and market disruptions, namely, even if they could sell troubled assets and new equity participations at prices reflecting fundamental values.

MARKET-BASED MECHANISMS FOR PURCHASING ASSETS AT FAIR MARKET VALUE

The plan I am putting forward would authorize the government to use public funds both to purchase troubled assets, as the Treasury plan suggests, and to purchase newly issued securities by financial firms in need of additional capital. Both types of purchases should be at fair market value. The devil, however, is in the details. How would the government know whether it is purchasing assets at fair market value and avoiding overpaying for assets at taxpayers' expense?

The proposed legislation allows the Treasury to conduct purchases through in-house operations, outside delegation, or any other method it chooses. It would be best, however, to direct the Treasury to operate through agents with strong market incentives.

Suppose that the economy has illiquid mortgage assets with a face value of $1,000 billion, and that the Treasury believes that the introduction of buyers armed with $100 billion could bring the necessary liquidity to this market. The Treasury could divide the $100 billion into, say, twenty funds of $5 billion and place each fund under a manager verified to have no conflicting interests. Each manager could be promised a fee equal to, say, 5 percent of the profit its fund generates—that is, the excess of the fund's final value down the road over the $5 billion of initial investment. The competition among these twenty funds would prevent the price paid for the mortgage assets from falling below fair value, and the fund managers' profit incentives would prevent the price from exceeding fair value.

The above example is intended to illustrate the point, of course, rather than to suggest particular details for the fee structure of the funds' managers. It would be necessary to determine the percentage of profits granted to managers and the threshold above which this percentage would be applied. One could consider taking the competitive idea one additional step: after a pool of candidates that pass threshold conditions in terms of expertise and lack of conflicting interests is selected, the selection could be based on a bidding process in which candidates would bid the profit percentage for which they would be willing to manage a fund.

Given that the decentralized system I am describing is far from straightforward, let me explain why it might nonetheless be preferable to having the government conduct purchases of a given class of assets through a single buyer, possibly located in-house in the Treasury. Certainly a situation in which a Treasury in-house official bargained one-on-one with a financial firm over the value of an asset would raise serious concerns. The Treasury's statement sought to allay these concerns by raising the possibility of using market mechanisms such as auctions or reverse auctions.

Suppose that the Treasury seeks to purchase some units within a certain class of assets—say, trench C in mortgage pool M. Under one possible procedure described by Chairman Bernanke in congressional testimony, the Treasury could name a price it is willing to pay per unit, based on its estimate of the hold-to-maturity value of these units, and financial firms would then decide to sell. But estimating accurately the hold-to-maturity value requires making estimates of the incidence of mortgage repayment years down the road, and it would be rather difficult for a Treasury official—or for those reviewing the official's decisions—to know whether the estimate made by the official is close to or far from accuracy. Indeed, it would be difficult to know this even in retrospect; if hold-to-maturity returns fall below the price paid, this might be due to the negative realization of uncertainty rather than to the use of an estimate that was too low when made.

Moreover, the Treasury official would face private actors with powerful incentives to maximize their interests. Thus even if Treasury officials are as likely to err in one direction as in the other in making their estimates, the result would be systematic overpaying for assets, for sellers would be more likely to accept the price named by the Treasury for units of trench C of pool M when the price is set too high and less likely to do so when the price is set too low.

An alternative procedure that a centralized one-buyer process could use would specify not the price that the Treasury is willing to pay for units in the class of assets but the number of units it is seeking to acquire—say, 50 percent of the units. The Treasury would then invite owners of units to submit offers as to the price at which they are willing to sell such assets, and it would purchase units at whatever level is sufficient to induce sale offers for the 50 percent of the units. In theory, this could work when ownership of units in this class of assets is dispersed among owners that cannot effectively coordinate the prices they would demand. However, in situations in which assets are owned by a concentrated group or by repeat players that can implicitly coordinate strategies, such auctions may produce inflated prices.

MANDATING RIGHTS OFFERINGS

My discussion thus far assumed, following the assumption underlying the Treasury's plan, that, because capital markets "froze," new capital infusions to financial firms need, at least to a substantial degree, to come from the government. However, financial firms that are undercapitalized but clearly solvent, as many financial firms seem to be, should be able to raise significant additional capital from private sources. It should be emphasized that the government has thus far not exhausted its options in terms of inducing financial firms to raise additional capital from private sources.

Following the Bear Stearns collapse in March, the government urged and encouraged some financial firms to raise additional capital. However, the government has not thus far required financial firms to go out and raise additional capital, and it should do so. As was suggested by Raghuram Rajan in a recent op-ed piece in the *Financial Times* (Rajan 2008), the government could and should require financial firms that have substantial but suboptimal capitalization to raise capital through rights offerings to existing shareholders. While such rights offerings would not be effective for firms in relatively fragile situations, they could bring significant additional capital to firms that are clearly solvent; this would substantially increase the aggregate capital available to the financial sector and, in turn, expand the pool of credit available to Main Street. There can be little doubt that if, say, Bank of America were required to make a rights offering at a price significantly below its current market price, the offering would be fully subscribed, would bring in significant additional capital, and hence would expand the capacity of this bank to provide financing to the real economy.

Because the proposed legislation is partly motivated by a concern that the financial sector's undercapitalization might undermine its ability to finance Main Street, mandating such rights offerings would contribute substantially to addressing this concern. Furthermore, it would do so at no cost to taxpayers. Thus, mandating rights offerings for an appropriate subset of the country's financial firms should be a useful supplement to (and partial substitute for) the use of public funds for these purposes.

The case for mandating rights offerings might be questioned on grounds that firms can, of course, choose on their own to raise new equity capital through rights offerings or otherwise. A mandate would necessarily be harmful in situations in which a firm on its own would choose not to do a rights offering, so the argument goes, and would be unnecessary in situations in which firms would choose to do so on their own. But this critique should not be accepted, for two reasons.

To begin, as pointed out by Rajan (2008), a "lemons" problem—in particular, fear of negative informational inferences that the market may draw from a decision to make a rights offering—might discourage a firm from doing so even if it needs capital. In contrast, when a rights offering is mandated by the government for a substantial set of firms, the market will not draw a negative inference about the managers' private information from the existence of a rights offering. Furthermore, the premise of the Treasury's plan is that the existence of adequate capitalization in given financial firms has substantial positive spillover effects on other firms in the economy. The existence of such effects might well make it desirable in the current circumstances to expand the capital available to financial firms even if financial firms' existing shareholders would privately prefer not to do so in order to avoid diluting their earnings.

CONCLUSION

Because the Treasury's plan would infuse capital through overpaying for troubled assets, it would impose massive costs on taxpayers and might not channel needed capital to its most valuable uses. The proposal put forward in this chapter would do a far better job both in terms of protecting taxpayers and in terms of restoring financial stability.

Because I focus here on the financial sector problems that the Treasury proposal seeks to address, I have abstracted from the problem of the housing market. It is generally recognized that the financial sector's problems are in part due to the "correction" in the housing market. Nonetheless, the assumption underlying the Treasury's plan is that government intervention should focus on the financial sector. The Treasury (now) recognizes that the problems of the financial markets should not be left to the market to sort out but, rather, require government intervention. However, once this intervention brings stability and liquidity to financial firms, the Treasury believes, the problems of the housing market can still be left for market forces to sort out. Unfortunately, however, the housing market is not a Coasian setting in which such adjustments can occur without much cost. Thus additional government intervention in connection with the housing market may be warranted alongside the intervention in the financial markets that has been the focus of this short treatment. Whether and what intervention would be warranted is a question that is beyond the scope of this chapter, however, and I plan to consider it in a separate work.

REFERENCES AND FURTHER READING

Edlin, Aaron. 2008. "Questioning the Treasury's $700 Billion Blank Check: An Open Letter to Secretary Paulson." *The Economists' Voice* 5, no. 5: art. 4. Available at www.bepress.com/ev/vol5/iss5/art4.

Rajan, Raghuram. 2008. "Desperate Times Need the Right Measures." *FT.com*, September 19. Available at http://blogs.ft.com/economists forum/2008/09/desperate-times-need-the-right-measures/#axzz1p PZzzF00.

U.S. Treasury Department. 2008. Proposed legislation. Available at www.bepress.com/cgi/viewcontent.cgi?context=ev&article=1408 &filename=0&type=additional.

CHAPTER 22

Please Think This Over

Edward E. Leamer

HERE ARE SOME choice words from the Treasury:

> Legislative Proposal for Treasury Authority
> to Purchase Mortgage-Related Assets
>
> The Secretary is authorized to purchase, and to make and fund commitments to purchase, on such terms and conditions as determined by the Secretary, mortgage-related assets from any financial institution having its headquarters in the United States.
>
> Decisions by the Secretary pursuant to the authority of this Act are non-reviewable and committed to agency discretion, and may not be reviewed by any court of law or any administrative agency.

Edward E. Leamer is the Chauncey J. Medberry Professor of Management, Professor of Economics and Statistics, and Director of the UCLA Anderson Forecast, all at UCLA. In addition, he was a member of Governor Arnold Schwarzenegger's Council of Economic Advisors.

When I first read those words in an e-mail, I thought it was an Internet joke. I was sure the Treasury Secretary would be explaining exactly how he would acquire these assets, since the devil is in the details. Instead, the Secretary wants authority to do whatever he wants. He doesn't even give us a mission statement, or any metrics for the success of this venture.

MY QUESTIONS

I have lots of questions about this, and I am sure you have many more:

- How is the Treasury going to determine the values of those illiquid mortgage-backed securities when Wall Street has failed to do so? Surely their values depend on future home prices and future mortgage default rates. How is the Treasury going to forecast home prices and default rates? Will these forecasts be made public?
- How is the Treasury going to avoid the winner's curse, paying more for these assets than anyone else is willing to? How can this plan help the financial institutions unless the Treasury does pay more for these securities than their current private market auction value, and even more than their current book value, thus in effect making a capital infusion into the banking system?
- Isn't there a big risk here of exposing rather than eliminating insolvency problems? Aren't some insolvency problems currently hidden with mark-to-model accounting valuations for these illiquid assets? When the Treasury creates a market for these assets, don't standard accounting rules require valuations at market prices, which will cause accounting losses for these firms unless the Treasury is more generous than the firms' accountants?

- Is the Treasury going to buy these securities from firms that are well capitalized and don't need the help as well as from firms that are on the brink of insolvency?
- Is the plan a way to rescue the mismanaged firms and keep the poorly performing management in place? If it doesn't do that, what help can the plan offer?
- What exactly is the definition of a "financial institution" from which the Treasury will buy mortgage-backed securities? Does it include pension funds and mutual funds? How about the loan I gave my neighbor that he now refuses to pay back? Am I a financial institution? I would like to be included in this too. Curiously the legislation does not define "financial institution," although it does define the "United States."
- How much in losses from this speculative enterprise can taxpayers reasonably expect? What systems will be put in place to limit the losses? Who will be held accountable for losses that exceed the limit? Who besides the taxpayers will have skin in the game?
- Why not just make a one-time federal capital infusion into all the troubled banks and let them do with the mortgage-backed securities whatever they like? That would leave the corpses in the hands of those who know where they are buried, as Steve Liesman recently pointed out on *Meet the Press*. Wouldn't that be a more honest and more efficient way of doing this bailout? Or maybe we should just nationalize the whole banking system? (I don't mean that!)
- Perhaps most importantly, have we thought at all about the unintended consequences of this government intervention into the capital markets? The Secretary pays a lot of lip service to the moral hazard problem, but a much bigger one is the pound of flesh. Don't think for a minute that Wall Street can walk away with $700 billion of the taxpayers' money without

draconian consequences. We may be opening up a regulation nightmare that will make Sarbanes-Oxley look like a walk in the park.

But the Treasury offered no details. Absolutely none. So we are left to guess. Given that the Treasury has had months (not days) to plan this, I hope (but I fear too) that it is simply not telling us its plans.

Didn't we just do this? Didn't we rush pell-mell to solve a huge problem, giving open-ended authority to our executive branch, only later to wish we had thought it over more carefully? Do we really want to give the Secretary of the Treasury $700 billion to do as he or she sees fit?

I don't like this half-baked plan. I don't think it is going to work. I don't think it addresses the root problems. Worst of all, it shakes the very foundations of our government's relationship with the private sector, setting us on a completely new course in what may be a politically irreversible way.

THE REAL PROBLEM AND A BETTER PLAN

Here is my take on the problems we face and what the proper treatments are. I offer these thoughts not because I know for sure. Mostly I want to remind us all that there are other ways to spend $700 billion of the taxpayers' money. Let's talk about this. Let's not rush to get it done by Friday.

Looking backward, home buyers paid too much, and lenders wrote contracts that exposed them to the homeowners' losses. With home values declining by something like $2 trillion, we are in a mad scramble to divide the loss between homeowners, lenders, and taxpayers. In the meantime, homeowners and lenders are exercising their last line of defense: denial. Many homeowners are refusing to sell their homes at prices that can attract buyers. Many lenders are refusing to sell their mortgage-backed securities at prices that can attract buyers. All this denial gets in the way of the normal price-discovery process, leaving stranded assets held by owners who think they are worth more than potential buyers.

Nonetheless, our financial institutions are doing a pretty good job. Our financial markets are supposed to tell us how wealthy we are. This year the large drop in equity valuations is sending a pretty clear message: we are not as wealthy as we thought. That seems adequately accurate; no big problem there. Our financial markets also provide credit to consumers and businesses to help grow our economy. Outside of housing, the economy is doing pretty well, and there is no clear evidence of a credit crunch seriously impinging on either business spending or consumer spending, even though Wall Street pundits for more than a year have been ringing out loud alarm bells about an imminent credit contraction. Though business spending and consumer spending are a bit weak, that weakness properly reflects the fundamentals of the economy and is not a symptom of a credit crunch. So what's the problem, Mr. Secretary?

I too am very worried about the next couple of quarters. We have not had the amplifying effect of massive layoffs, however, there are some ominous signs. But if business spending or consumer spending in the future is substantially curtailed by a credit contraction, couldn't we have a government program that directly encourages whatever spending problem shows up? If business spending weakens, could we try a tax credit for business investment? If jobs are declining, what about a tax credit for firms that hire more workers? Why this round-about doubtful solution that for sure helps the Secretary's friends on Wall Street and maybe not much else?

We all need to understand that the "root" problem isn't bad mortgages, as the Treasury Secretary and the president allege; the root problem is declining home prices, caused by a combination of overbuilding and excessive appreciation, together with aggressive mortgages that only work when prices are rising rapidly. To formulate an appropriate response we need first to form an opinion regarding the amount of overbuilding and the amount of home price declines that are likely to occur in the future and the rates of foreclosure that will occur at those prices. The values of those mortgage-backed securities that Secretary Paulson is so anxious to buy on our behalf depend completely on the future foreclosure rates and on the future underlying values of the foreclosed homes that taxpayers soon enough will own. What can be expected with regard to prices and home building?

High rates of home building from 2004 to 2006 gave us about a million more single-family homes than suggested by historical rates of building, illustrated in Figure 22.1. Since 2006, plummeting rates of building have reduced that home overhang to about 400,000 units, and we should be back on trend in the stock of homes very early in 2009. (As it turned out, cumulative single-family home building was back to trend in February 2009, but continuing low rates of building through August 2011 have produced a deficit of single-family homes of 2.1 million units and a deficit of multi-family

FIGURE 22.1

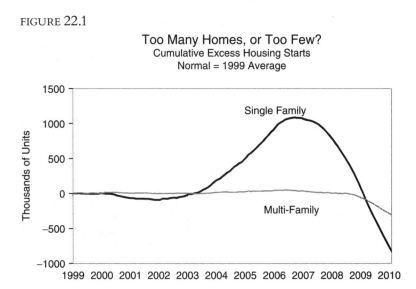

Too Many Homes, or Too Few?
Cumulative Excess Housing Starts
Normal = 1999 Average

homes of 880,000 units, thus laying the foundation for the next housing boom.)

A rough calculation of the remaining excess in home prices can be made by extending the 1975–2002 inflation-adjusted trend in the Federal Housing Finance Agency home price index to 2008q2 and comparing that with the actual index. That suggests a remaining over-valuation of 24 percent, illustrated in Figure 22.2. Using the 2008q2 rate of decline in home prices, –5 percent, and the inflation rate of 2 percent, it will take a little less than three years for home prices to get back to trend. It seems likely going forward that the inflation rate will be higher and the rate of home price decline greater. It is also the case that some of the excess is a consequence of the low rate of interest. Still, it doesn't seem reasonable to expect this pricing problem to be solved nationwide before the end of 2009, at the earliest, when home prices are likely to be down another 10 percent at least. (As it turned out, it was in

FIGURE 22.2

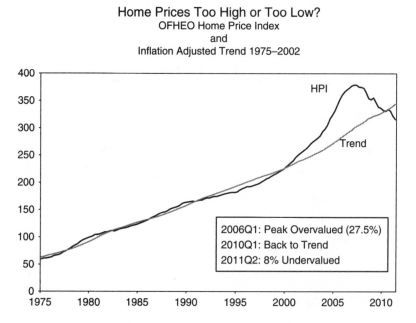

Home Prices Too High or Too Low?
OFHEO Home Price Index
and
Inflation Adjusted Trend 1975–2002

2006Q1: Peak Overvalued (27.5%)
2010Q1: Back to Trend
2011Q2: 8% Undervalued

the first quarter of 2010 when home prices returned to trend, and in the second quarter are below trend by 8 percent).

The data thus suggest that the overbuilding problem is going to be behind us early next year, when the stock of single-family homes will be back to normal, but the price declines for new and existing homes are likely to go on for at least another year or two.

Those declining home prices are going to cause more losses for homeowners, lenders, and taxpayers. Taxpayers need to decide how much of those losses they are prepared to absorb, if any, and they need to put in place mechanisms that will directly and clearly transfer the losses from homeowners to taxpayers. The Paulson plan transfers to taxpayers an indeterminate level of losses buried already in the books of the lenders. I cannot see how that helps homeowners at all, except for the argument that it averts a severe credit contraction that might make life miserable for all of us. Surely we can think of cheaper, more direct, and more effective ways to deal with any excessive credit contraction that does emerge.

One honest way to transfer the losses directly to the taxpayers would have the Treasury buy homes directly at inflated prices and rent them to deserving Americans. Though the Treasury Plan involves buying mortgage-backed securities at inflated prices, keep in mind that foreclosures will then turn the homes over to Uncle Sam. For $700 billion, the Treasury could purchase 2.3 million homes at an average price of $300,000. That is way more than is necessary. A half a million should be enough to unclog the system. Uncle Sam could purchase foreclosed homes, mow the lawns, fix the broken windows, and rent the homes out to deserving families. That would help the other homes in the neighborhood sell at favorable prices.

The overbuilding problem will be corrected long before prices stabilize, but the continuing decline in home prices will make it impossible to build the homes we need, and the consequent underbuilding will lay the foundation for the next housing mania. To get the builders up and running early next year, we need a tax rebate for the purchase of new homes, beginning soon.

When prices get back in line with fundamentals, there are likely to be continuing price declines because the housing market works pathologically. A normal market works because demand curves are downward sloping, but for homes demand curves can be upward sloping. Declining prices in many regions are not bringing buyers back to the market. Price declines are creating the expectation of more price declines to come and encouraging prospective buyers to postpone their decisions, which causes more price declines and eventually the overshooting of prices. When prices get back to normal and buyers have not returned, that's when we need to find ways to bring the buyers back. That's when we need to offer big temporary tax credits to first-time buyers.

So that's my $700 billion plan.

Immediate relief for homeowners who don't like the price the market is offering.

1. Have Uncle Sam do the buying. (If that sounds ridiculous, think again about the Paulson Plan.)
2. Offer a tax rebate for the purchase of new homes, commencing in January 2010.
3. Offer a temporary tax rebate for first-time buyers of either new or existing homes that is timed differently in different regions of the United States.

By the way, this plan might actually indirectly solve some of the problems that Paulson's friends on Wall Street are worried about—a kind of trickle-up economics.

CHAPTER 23

Is Macroeconomics Off Track?

Casey B. Mulligan

SHOULD MACROECONOMISTS BEGIN again, particularly those at Chicago, Minnesota, Rochester, and other freshwater schools? These days, commentators tell us that we should scrap all that we hold dear— neoclassical growth models, asset pricing models, and the efficient market hypothesis alike.

And not just run-of-the-mill journalists. No less than the Nobel Laureate Paul Krugman argued this September 2, 2009, in the *New York Times Sunday Magazine* that we are "mistaking beauty for truth," dismissing "the Keynesian vision of what recessions are all about," falling "in love with the vision of perfect markets," and blaming entire recessions on laziness.

Krugman and others are getting carried away. Allow me to defend neoclassical growth models by providing some examples of the application of these models to the current recession, and to previous

Casey B. Mulligan is a Professor of Economics at the University of Chicago. He writes a daily blog, www.panic2008.net, that applies the principles of supply and demand to today's recession.

recessions. The reader can then evaluate whether Krugman's accusations are at all accurate.

THE NEOCLASSICAL GROWTH MODEL

The neoclassical growth model is an aggregate model with two basic trade-offs: (1) current versus future and (2) market versus non-market allocations of labor. Resources are allocated over time via decisions to accumulate a homogeneous capital good rather than consuming in the current period. People allocate their time between the market and non-market sectors via employment and hours decisions.

The model has a few equilibrium conditions. Three conditions, denoted (Y), (L), and (K), relate to current consumption and work: (Y) output is produced according to capital and labor inputs, (L) the supply of labor equals its demand, and (K) the supply of capital (consumption foregone) equals its demand. The remaining two conditions are versions of (Y) and (L) for the future period.

Stated this way, the model seems to be based on the assumption that markets always clear. But twenty years of applying the model has not exactly been a love affair with perfect markets. My practice, and others', is to include a residual in each of the conditions: a "productivity shock" in condition (Y), a "labor market distortion" in condition (L), and an "investment" or a "capital market distortion" in condition (K), which means that I expect there may be significant market imperfections or other unpredictabilities.[1] The not-so-subtle truth is that we often suspect that markets are not functioning efficiently: one of my papers on the topic is titled "A Century of Labor-Leisure Distortions."[2]

Three Diagnostics

In its most basic form the neoclassical growth model has neither money nor fiscal policy. Nevertheless, it provides some diagnostics as to how public policy variables might be affecting the private sector.

In this approach the first step uses the macroeconomic data to suggest which of the conditions—(Y), (L), or (K)—has the most variable residual. Much like microeconomists ask "Was it supply or demand?"(as Lawrence Katz and Kevin Murphy [1992] have done with changes in relative wages), we users of the neoclassical growth model ask "Was it productivity? Labor supply? Labor demand? Capital supply? Capital demand?" We doubt that the complexity of the larger economy will ever be understood without some means of compartmentalizing the various behaviors, and the three "equilibrium conditions" are our means of doing so.

While a variety of tools would be appropriate for understanding the roles of monetary and fiscal policy, the neoclassical growth model's decomposition offers some suggestions as to which approaches might help the most. For example, we might think differently about monetary policy if it depressed the labor market by inadvertently raising real wages rather than depressing capital accumulation by adding frictions to capital markets.

NOT ALL RECESSIONS ARE THE SAME

Well before the current recession began, this approach led to the conclusion that recessions have various causes and, therefore, that no one government policy could fix all recessions or be blamed for all of them.

I have long been of the opinion that the labor supply residual, rather than productivity or investment shocks, was the most important of the three residuals in the Great Depression.[3] Despite the current recession's *capital* market theatrics, it again seems that much of the action is with the *labor* supply residual.

For the periods 1929–1933 and 2008–2009, labor supply residuals seem key because employment was low while total factor productivity and real pre-tax wages were high (or, in the period 1929–1933, at least not commensurately low). My story, then, is not so different from the business cycle described by General-Theory Keynes (see Keynes 1936) himself.

In this regard, results like mine, and those in recent works by Lee Ohanian (2009), Robert Shimer (2009), and Robert Hall (2009), are quite consistent with "the Keynesian vision of what recessions are all about": *something* made real wages high and employment low. But long ago we recognized that many other recessions cannot be characterized that way: real wages and employment frequently cycle together, as Mark Bils (1985) has found. In these other cases the "productivity shock" emphasized in the seminal work of Finn Kydland and Edward Prescott (1982) seems to be pretty important. There was a good reason old-time Keynesian models fell into disrepute soon after the 1970s stagflation.

Examination of Incentives

Given the recent time series for real wages and productivity, I doubt many of us are looking for an adverse productivity shock. But we do ask how individual incentives might be consistent with those patterns. It's this type of reasoning that led Lee Ohanian (2009) to blame some of the Great Depression on Hoover's industrial policy.

When it came to this recession, the neoclassical decomposition quickly led me to look further at public policies—absent from some of the other recessions—that might have caused the supply of labor to shift relative to its demand. Like others, I noticed that the federal minimum wage was hiked three consecutive times. I also turned up a major policy (the Treasury and the Federal Deposit Insurance Corporation plans for modifying mortgages) that creates marginal income tax rates in excess of 100 percent.[4] Much research remains to be done, and undoubtedly other users of the neoclassical growth model will make convincing cases for the roles of monetary and other factors.

Paul Krugman's scorn is all we have to suggest that marginal tax rates in excess of 100 percent are not worthy of attention and that today's low employment is not even partly a consequence of public policy. But regardless of how economists ultimately interpret today's recession, it will be notable for the basic fact that total factor productivity advanced while employment fell, and for the initial reception suffered by the basic facts in a politicized marketplace for ideas.

NOTES

1. See Parkin 1988, Mulligan 2005, and Chari, Kehoe, and McGrattan 2007, and the references cited therein; see Barro and King 1984 and Hall 1997 for early emphasis on the labor residual.

2. See also Gali, Gertler, and Lopez-Salido 2007.

3. Mulligan 2002; 2005. Well before this recession began, the basic methodology of neoclassical growth model residual analysis had been repeatedly applied even to the Great Depression, as in Cole and Ohanian 1999; 2004; Prescott 1999; the various papers in Kehoe and Prescott 2007; and Ohanian 2009.

4. Mulligan 2008; 2009a.

REFERENCES AND FURTHER READING

Barro, Robert J., and Robert G. King. 1984. "Time Separable Preferences and Intertemporal Substitution Models of Business Cycles." *Quarterly Journal of Economics* 99, no. 4: 817–39. Available at www.jstor.org/pss/1883127.

Bils, Mark. 1985. "Real Wages Over the Business Cycle; Evidence from Panel Data." *Journal of Political Economy* 93, no. 4: 666–89. Available at www.jstor.org/pss/1832132.

Chari, V. V., Patrick J. Kehoe, and Ellen R. McGrattan. 2007. "Business Cycle Accounting." *Econometrica* 75, no. 3: 781–836. Available at www.jstor.org/stable/4502010.

Cole, Harold L., and Lee E. Ohanian. 1999. "The Great Depression in the United States from a Neoclassical Perspective." *Federal Reserve*

Bank of Minneapolis Quarterly Review 23, no. 1: 2–24. Available at www.minneapolisfed.org/research/QR/QR2311.pdf.

Cole, Harold L., and Lee E. Ohanian. 2004. "New Deal Policies and the Persistence of the Great Depression: A General Equilibrium Analysis." *Journal of Political Economy* 112, no. 4: 779–816. Available at www .econ.yale.edu/seminars/echist/eh02/ohanian-021008.pdf.

Gali, Jordi, Mark Gertler, and J. David Lopez-Salido. 2007. "Markups, Gaps, and the Welfare Costs of Business Fluctuations." *Review of Economics and Statistics* 89: 44–59. Available at www.nyu.edu/econ /user/gertlerm/gap42.pdf.

Hall, Robert E. 1997. "Macroeconomic Fluctuations and the Allocation of Time." *Journal of Labor Economics* 15, no. 1: S223–50. Available at www.nber.org/papers/w5933.

Hall, Robert E. 2009. "Reconciling Cyclical Movements in the Marginal Value of Time and the Marginal Product of Labor." *Journal of Political Economy* 117, no. 2: 281–323. Available at www.journals .uchicago.edu/doi/abs/10.1086/599022.

Katz, Lawrence F., and Kevin M. Murphy. 1992. "Changes in Relative Wages, 1963–1987: Supply and Demand Factors." *Quarterly Journal of Economics* 107, no. 1: 35–78. Available at www.jstor.org/pss/2118323.

Kehoe, Timothy J., and Edward C. Prescott. 2007. *Great Depressions of the Twentieth Century.* Minneapolis, Minn.: Federal Reserve Bank of Minneapolis.

Keynes, John Maynard. 1936. *The General Theory of Employment, Interest, and Money.* London: Macmillan. (Diagnosing on p. 17 the 1929–1933 period in a way similar to my own diagnosis.)

Kydland, Finn, and Edward C. Prescott. 1982. "Time to Build and Aggregate Fluctuations." *Econometrica* 50, no. 6: 1345–70. Available at www.minneapolisfed.org/research/prescott/papers/timetobuild.pdf.

Mulligan, Casey B. 2002. "A Century of Labor-Leisure Distortions." NBER Working Paper No. 8774, February. Available at www.nber .org/papers/w8774.pdf.

Mulligan, Casey B. 2005. "Public Policies as Specification Errors." *Review of Economic Dynamics* 8, no. 4: 902–26. Available at http://bit.ly/4lKn1j.

Mulligan, Casey B. 2008. "A Depressing Scenario: Mortgage Debt Becomes Unemployment Insurance." NBER Working Paper No. 14514. Available at www.nber.org/papers/w14514.

Mulligan, Casey B. 2009a. "Means-Tested Mortgage Modification: Homes Saved or Income Destroyed." NBER Working Paper No. 15821. Available at www.nber.org/papers/w15281.

Mulligan, Casey B. 2009b. "What Caused the Recession of 2008? Hints from Labor Productivity." NBER Working Paper No. 14729. Available at www.nber.org/papers/w14729.

Ohanian, Lee E. 2009. "What—or Who—Started the Great Depression?" *Journal of Economic Theory*. 144, no. 6 (November): 2310–35. Available at http://ic.ucsc.edu/~fravenna/appliedmacro/lucas_confer_final_berkeley.pdf.

Parkin, Michael. 1988. "A Method for Determining Whether Parameters in Aggregative Models Are Structural." In *Money, Cycles, and Exchange Rates: Essays in Honor of Allan H. Meltzer*. Allan H. Meltzer, Karl Brunner, and Bennett T. McCallum, ed. Carnegie-Rochester Conference Series on Public Policy 29: 215–52.

Prescott, Edward C. 1999. "Some Observations on the Great Depression." *Federal Reserve Bank of Minneapolis Quarterly Review* 23, no. 1: 25–31. Available at www.minneapolisfed.org/research/QR/QR2312.pdf.

Shimer, Robert. 2009. *Labor Markets and Business Cycles*. Princeton, N.J.: Princeton University Press.

CHAPTER 24

If It Were a Fight, They Would Have Stopped It in December of 2008

Robert J. Barbera

IN THE DECEMBER 2009 issue of *The Economists' Voice*, University of Chicago Professor Casey Mulligan (see Mulligan 2009) rejected Paul Krugman's rebuke of freshwater economics and reaffirmed his faith in the New Classical Economics. His defense was short. He offered up a super-stylized macro model and pointed out that inclusion of a distortion term for his capital and labor market equilibrium conditions allowed him to comfortably explain the 2008–2009 recession. Really?

As a Wall Street economic practitioner, I am decidedly unconvinced. Practitioners and theorists, I think, are in agreement that a theory is supposed to help us understand how the world works. If a theory of gravity concludes that apples freed from trees tend to float to the heavens, one need not understand the math to reject the

Robert J. Barbera is a Fellow of the Economics Department at Johns Hopkins University. He is also the author of *The Cost of Capitalism: Market Mayhem and Stabilizing Our Economic Future* (New York: McGraw Hill, 2009).

construct. And that is why, after the brutal events of 2008–2009, I naïvely thought we would be able to end debate about the plausibility of real business cycle theory.

It is worth looking back at Professor Mulligan's (see Mulligan 2008) op-ed piece in the *New York Times* from October 9, 2008. There, Professor Mulligan dismissed the notion of contagion in the financial sector. He looked for pension funds, university endowments, and newly created and capitalized banks to fill the lending gap:

> Although banks perform an essential economic function—bringing together investors and savers—they are not the only institutions that can do this. Pension funds, university endowments, venture capitalists and corporations all bring money to new investment projects without banks playing any essential role. The average corporation gets about a quarter of its investment funds from the profits it has after paying dividends—and could double or even triple that amount by cutting its dividend, if necessary.
>
> What's more, it's not as if banking services are about to vanish. When a bank or a group of banks go under, the economy-wide demand for their services creates a strong profit motive for new banks to enter the marketplace and for existing banks to expand their operations. (Bank of America and J. P. Morgan Chase are already doing this.)

He went on to dismiss the importance of financial market gyrations:

> Economic research has repeatedly demonstrated that financial-sector gyrations like these are hardly connected to non-financial sector performance. Studies have shown that economic growth cannot be forecast by the expected rates of return on government bonds, stocks or savings deposits.

A much better predictive tool, he asserted, was the marginal product of capital:

> When the profit per dollar of capital invested in the economy is higher than average, future rates of economic growth also tend to be above average. The same cannot be said about rates of return on the S&P 500, or any other measurement that commands attention on Wall Street.

He pointed out that "the marginal product of capital was more than 10 percent per year." Strong gains for the marginal product of capital thus favored good growth in 2009.

The crisis in banks, Professor Mulligan concluded, was really only a concern for the hapless few who work for banks:

> So, if you are not employed by the financial industry (94 percent of you are not), don't worry. The current unemployment rate of 6.1 percent is not alarming, and we should reconsider whether it is worth it to spend $700 billion to bring it down to 5.9 percent.

REALITY CHECK

The facts on the ground, however, refused to cooperate. In the fourth quarter of 2008, as Professor Mulligan penned his words, 1.68 million payroll jobs were lost, and the unemployment rate jumped by a full percentage point, to 7.2 percent. Needless to say, more than 90 percent of the job losers worked outside the financial sector. All of this carnage was already looming when Professor Mulligan wrote his *Times* essay. The conclusion I am forced to come to is that the new classical economics framework seems to be an impediment not only to prediction but to description.

To be sure, a single forecasting error is not sufficient grounds to dismiss either a framework or a forecaster. Indeed, if getting a prediction wrong was all it took for dismissal, the unemployment rate among forecasters would be awfully close to 100 percent. At the same time, if unwavering faith in a framework blinds you to both the potential for crisis and to its actual *arrival,* you have a big problem.

Worse still, if you and your framework have the ear of policy makers, you might well become a problem for all of us. To put it bluntly, it is dangerous to pretend that bank runs cannot happen—especially when you are knee deep in one.

Isn't it reasonable for *all economists* to acknowledge that the events of the past year were a whopping big *natural experiment*? In the aftermath of the failed Lehman Brothers rescue effort, two very distinct story lines appeared. Shouldn't we all care about which narrative carried the day?

Keynesian economists, comfortable with the elaborations of Hyman Minsky and Charles Kindleberger, declared in late 2008 that we were experiencing a *Minsky moment.* The signs were there: bank run dynamics in the repo market and a collapsing commercial paper market. Panic hoarding of cash by companies on Main Street was destined to follow. This would produce a slashing of orders and a sharp rise in joblessness. A massive bank rescue effort might well prevent a depression from happening again, but a tough recession was baked in the cake.

New Classical economists could not have disagreed more. "Forget the banks," they explained; pension funds and insurance companies will wisely step in and prevent a contagion. Companies will continue to see their profits rise and will be comfortable depending on internally generated funds for working capital. Economists need only focus on the heady marginal product of capital in place in 2007 and 2008. On that basis they should be willing to argue that 2009 would surprise on the upside. Faith in unfettered markets and the New Classical tradition would be rewarded when 2009 turns out to be fine.

NOT A PRETTY PICTURE

The results, of course, have come in.

A modern-day bank run unfolded in the repo market. The contagion infected risky asset markets in areas far removed from housing or banking. Pension funds, university endowments, and banks were engulfed in the crisis and in no mood to step up as lenders. Companies hoarded cash and were universally unwilling to depend on internally generated funds. The result was a global plunge of activity and employment. A worldwide rescue of banks ensued; and then, in classic Kindlebergian form, an unmistakable revival in risky asset markets; and, most recently, signs of economic recovery.

Professor Mulligan, of course, interprets the past year very differently. Undaunted by his fantastic forecasting error, his December 2009 essay recasts the story of the period 2008–2009. For Mulligan, notwithstanding "the current recession's capital market theatrics . . . much of the action is with the labor supply residual." What caused the labor supply shock? Mulligan notes "that the minimum wage was hiked three consecutive times." But the important point to remember, as I see it, is not what Professor Mulligan asserted last month but instead what he counseled in late 2008. Sadly for him and for all of us, everything he expected to happen did not come to pass. Everything he dismissed as unlikely actually happened in spades.

Am I missing something? I am sure that many real-business-cycle zealots think I have missed almost everything. But for the majority of economists, those who use theory to try and make sense of the world, shouldn't we all agree that the New Classical framework failed in spectacular fashion last year?

IRRATIONAL EXUBERANCE

For me, the hard part in all of this is to figure out how anyone is still willing to make a *rational* case for New Classical Economics. My best explanation arrives via my own experience as a baseball fan. I have been a Mets fan since 1963, surrounded by an extended family of Yankee fans. This exercise in masochism has caused me untoward humiliation and embarrassment for decades. But my commitment occurred in my formative years, and I just can't bring myself to acknowledge the long-standing and readily observable superiority of the Yankee tradition. It is not rational for me to remain a Mets fan, but my emotional attachment wins out over my rational self.

Is it rational for real-business-cycle enthusiasts to defend a model that missed the biggest economic event of our lifetimes? Or are emotions getting the better of them?

REFERENCES AND FURTHER READING

Barbera, Robert J., and Charles L. Weise. 2008. "It's the Right Moment to Embrace the Minsky Model." In *The Elgar Companion to Hyman Minsky*, ed. Dimitri B. Papadimitriou and L. Randall Wray. Williston, Vt.: Edward Elgar Publishing. Available at http://econ.jhu.edu/courses/336/.

Gorton, Gary, and Andrew Metrick. 2009. "Securitized Banking and the Run on Repo." Yale ICF Working Paper No. 09–14. Available at http://ssrn.com/abstract=1440752.

Mulligan, Casey. 2008. "An Economy You Can Bank On." *New York Times*. Available at www.nytimes.com/2008/10/10/opinion/10mulligan.html.

Mulligan, Casey. 2009. "Is Macroeconomics Off Track?" *The Economist's Voice* 6, no. 10: art. 6. Available at www.bepress.com/ev/vol6/iss10/art6/.

"Right Moment to Embrace the Minsky Model. Essay in Honor of Hyman Minsky." July 2008. In *The Elgar Companion to Hyman Minsky*, ed. Dimitri B. Papadimitriou and L. Randall Wray. Williston, Vt.: Edward Elgar Publishing. (This makes the case for giving elevated status to risky company asset prices when conducting monetary policy.)

Sterling, William. 2009. "Looking Back at Lehman: An Empirical Analysis of the Financial Shock and the Effectiveness of Counter-measures." *Musashi University Journal* 57, no. 2. Available at www.trilogyadvisors.com/worldreport/200910.Lehman.pdf. (This identifies the swings in risky company asset prices that confirm that the 2008–2009 crisis reflected panic about Lehman's bankruptcy, not concerns about government intrusion.)

Weise, Charles L., and Robert J. Barbera. 2008. "Minsky Meets Wicksell: Using the Wicksellian Model to Understand the Twenty-First Century Business Cycle." In *Macroeconomic Theory and Macroeconomic Pedagogy*, ed. Giuseppe Fontana and Mark Setterfield. Basingstoke and New York: Palgrave Macmillan. Available at www.gettysburg.edu/dotAsset/2104335.pdf. (This demonstrates that violent swings in risky company credit spreads drive boom/bust cycles and require an activist Central Bank.)

CHAPTER 25

Comment on Barbera: Your Gift Will Make You Rich

Casey B. Mulligan

DEAR EDITORS:

As the current recession was unfolding, Nobel Laureate Paul Krugman accused (Krugman 2009) modern macroeconomists of "mistaking beauty for truth," dismissing "the Keynesian vision of what recessions are all about," falling "in love with the vision of perfect markets," and blaming entire recessions on laziness.

I published an article in *The Economists' Voice* (Mulligan 2009) showing that Krugman's accusations were incorrect and pointing readers to a number of articles published by some of those modern macroeconomists. I also gave examples in which modern macroeconomists used the neoclassical growth model primarily to examine the market imperfections that we supposedly ignore, and how those established techniques were being applied to the current recession well before it was over.

Mr. Barbera appears to disagree with my article and to deeply dislike modern macroeconomics. His view is not based on a reading of the academic literature that is being debated, nor even a balanced examination of my own portfolio of economic research and forecasting but, rather, on just two observations: (1) that I and some of the other modern macroeconomists do not think that an interruption of activity in the banking sector (where Mr. Barbera works) is all that critical to the rest of the economy, and (2) that I made one incorrect forecast in October 2008.

Regarding my forecasts in 2008, it is true that I predicted in October that national nonfarm payroll employment would stay above 134 million, when later it would drop as low as 129.6 million. At the same time, I also predicted, correctly, that real GDP would not drop below $11 trillion (chained 2000 $). And already in my writings in November 2008 I began to appreciate that a plethora of new public policies was drastically eroding incentives for individuals to earn income and for businesses to employ people.

Yes, I was surprised that employment dropped so much. I agree with Mr. Barbera that the drop is, so far, "the biggest economic event of our lifetimes." But almost as newsworthy is the fact that U.S. employment would drop so much while real production and spending (i.e., GDP) would drop so little by comparison.

As I explained in my earlier article, these twin facts make it difficult to embrace Mr. Barbera's view that the banking crisis caused this recession to be so deep. Neither he nor Professor Krugman has shared with us any explanation of how a banking crisis would, by the end of 2009, pull down employment and hours 8 percent yet pull down real spending less than 5 percent (relative to the trend four years before the recession, these drops are 12 and 7 percent, respectively).[1] My article offered an explanation in terms of labor market distortions, and said that "undoubtedly other users of the neoclassical growth model will make convincing cases for the roles of monetary and other factors."

Let's not forget that taxpayers were forced to swallow a massive bank bailout on the grounds that even a short interruption of banking activity would be devastating, and bank bailout funds would be lent to consumers and businesses. Yet it is now widely recognized that the bailout funds did not increase lending.

Because labor and capital are complements in production, the facts that investment spending and corporate profits were low during the recession are not necessarily evidence that a bank lending collapse caused the recession, and fit well with my hypothesis that this recession is rooted in the labor market, not in Wall Street. Investment was low largely because labor usage was low, and the future seemed so uncertain. Even if banks were eager to lend, why should businesses purchase new capital goods when many of them had fewer employees and were not using much of their existing capital?

Nor are the facts that consumption spending and asset prices fell before most of this recession's job losses occurred necessarily evidence that the job losses were caused by either bank industry stress or changes in consumer spending patterns. Economists debate the efficiency of fluctuations in consumption and asset prices, but by now we all admit that these behaviors reflect, at least in part, expectations about the future. Even under my hypothesis that this recession was mainly due to problems in the labor market, the drops in consumption and asset prices would be among the first symptoms to be visible in the national economic data.

Recent events only reinforce the prescription that economic analysis should be rooted in incentives, not voodoo incantations of multipliers and contagion. But the latter will continue to enjoy prominence in the political marketplace, where there's nothing like telling taxpayers, "Give me your money and, trust me, your gift will make you richer."

Casey B. Mulligan
University of Chicago

NOTE

1. Employment and hours are the Bureau of Labor Statistics' Average Weekly Hours (AWHI) index, adjusted to include changes in public employment and aggregated to quarters. Real GDP is from the Bureau of Economic Analysis' quarterly series through 2009-IV.

REFERENCES AND FURTHER READING

Barbera, Robert J. 2010. "If It Were a Fight, They Would Have Stopped It in December of 2008." *The Economists' Voice* 7, no. 1: art. 3. Available at www.bepress.com/ev/vol7/iss2/art3.

Krugman, Paul. 2009. "How Did Economists Get It So Wrong?" *New York Times,* September 2. Available at www.nytimes.com/2009/09/06/magazine/06Economic-t.html.

Mulligan, Casey B. 2008a. "A Depressing Scenario: Mortgage Debt Becomes Unemployment Insurance." NBER Working Paper No. 14514, November. Available at www.nber.org/papers/w14514.

Mulligan, Casey B. 2008b. "Don't Forgive that Way!" *Chicago Tribune,* December 5. Available at http://articles.chicagotribune.com/2008-12-05/news/0812040799_1_family-income-income-tax-borrowers.

Mulligan, Casey B. 2008c. "An Economy You Can Bank On." *New York Times.* Available at www.nytimes.com/2008/10/10/opinion/10mulligan.html.

Mulligan, Casey B. 2009. "Is Macroeconomics Off Track?" *The Economists' Voice* 6, no. 10: art. 6. Available at www.bepress.comev/vol6/iss10/art6.

PART IV

INNOVATIONS IN POLICY AND BUSINESS

CHAPTER 26

Pension Security Bonds: A New Plan to Address the State Pension Crisis

Joshua Rauh and Robert Novy-Marx

THE FEDERAL GOVERNMENT should be worried about state pension liabilities. In the absence of fundamental reform, some large state pension funds may not last through this decade. When the funds run through their assets, the size of promised benefit payments will be so large that raising state taxes enough to make these pension payments will be infeasible. Just as the European Union is not standing back to watch Greece fail, the federal government will face massive and likely irresistible pressure to bail out the affected state governments.

Take Illinois, for example. Even if its main three pension funds earn 8 percent returns and the state makes enough contributions to secure new benefits in the coming years, those funds will run out of money in 2018. At that time, benefit payments owed to the workers who are already in today's state workforce will be an estimated

Joshua Rauh is Associate Professor of Finance at the Kellogg School of Management at Northwestern University and NBER. Robert Novy-Marx is Assistant Professor of Finance at the University of Chicago Booth School of Business and NBER.

$14 billion per year. That is half of the $28 billion in total general fund revenues that Illinois is expected to have received in 2010.

While this problem is particularly severe in states such as Illinois, Connecticut, and New Jersey, many more states have public pension systems that appear unsustainable even on a 15-year horizon (see Rauh 2010). The situation will be exacerbated if mobile taxpayers, frustrated with a large portion of their tax remittances going to pay pensioners, flee to states that can provide lower taxes and higher levels of service. The total size of the potential federal pension bailouts would likely exceed the recent bailout of the U.S. financial system.

When a country gets into fiscal trouble, the policy prescription is usually that it should implement fiscal austerity measures such as tax increases, spending cuts, and pension reforms. These measures essentially bring future budgets closer to balance and improve the country's solvency. The tighter budget also allows the country to borrow the large sums of money that will prevent the legacy liabilities from shutting down the government. The borrowing provides the country with the liquidity to keep operating.

In the case of the U.S. states, the legacy liabilities are the defined benefit (DB) pension promises to state and local government workers. Under a number of state constitutions, promised pension benefits have a legal priority that is senior even to general obligation bonds. States cannot simply back out of these payments. Troubled states that are interested in preventing a crisis should therefore take a page out of the book on sovereign fiscal crises. They should combine fiscal and pension reforms to improve solvency with increased borrowing to keep operating through the flood of benefit payments coming over the coming decades.

A key reform for states in pension trouble would be the closing of DB pension plans to new workers, an arrangement called a "soft freeze." Current employees would continue to earn traditional pension benefits under the existing programs, but retirement benefits for future workers would come under a new defined contribution (DC) plan. The Michigan State Employees Retirement System enacted such a policy for its new workers starting in 1998, although Michigan's systems for public school employees, state police, and judges still are exclusively DB and have about 460,000 members combined.

These changes must be enacted with an eye toward giving new public employees adequate retirement benefits. Those who are not in Social Security must be brought into Social Security, and the new DC plan must be adequate for supporting the retirement of public employees. The new plan must have automatic enrollment, matching employer contributions, low fees, good investment choices, sensible default allocations, and reasonably priced offers for annuities at retirement.

Once a state or municipal government has stopped unfunded pension liabilities from growing, it becomes more feasible, and less costly, for the state to issue debt to improve its liquidity situation.

A FEDERAL ROLE

If states were acting in our national interests, and indeed in their own long-term interests, they would be considering these actions themselves. Unfortunately, to the extent that state governments have taken action, it has been largely with cosmetic adjustments to existing systems. It therefore falls to the federal government to give states incentives for pension reform, so that U.S. taxpayers do not ultimately bear the burden of bailing out profligate states.

One area where incentives could be offered is through the treatment of bonds used to fund pensions. Under current law, bonds floated by states to fund pensions are fully taxable. As a result, issuing debt to fund pension plans is considerably more expensive than issuing regular tax-exempt municipal bonds, or the federally subsidized

Build America Bonds, on which the federal government reimburses 35 percent of all coupon payments directly to the state.

We propose that the federal government cut a deal with the states. A state should be allowed to issue tax-subsidized bonds for the purpose of pension funding for the next 15 years—if and only if the state government agrees to take three specific measures to stop the growth of unfunded liabilities:

1. The state must close its DB plans to new employees and agree not to start any new DB plans for at least 30 years;

2. The state must annually make its actuarially required contribution (ARC) left over from the existing DB plans; and

3. The state must include its new workers in Social Security and provide them with an adequate DC plan, again for at least 30 years. To this end, the federal government should start a Thrift Savings Program for state workers and operate it alongside the existing Thrift Savings Program for federal workers.

The tax subsidies for these new Pension Security Bonds would work like Build America Bonds, with the federal government paying 35 percent of coupon payments directly to the state. Only the amount of the ARC will be tax deductible, to prevent states from overfunding plans and to bring the bonds to the market gradually over 15 years.

HOW MUCH WILL IT COST?

State ARCs for fiscal year 2008 were approximately $67 billion, so the federal government is allowing potentially this much of new tax-exempt borrowing for each of the next 15 years. Assuming that the growth of the ARC is no greater than the discount rate that should be used to discount them, the plan would bring $1.0 trillion (= $67 billion × 15 years) in debt to the market. There is some risk of higher ARC growth in the first several years of the plan, but the fact that fewer and fewer workers will be on the DB plans will limit the ARC growth.

If states issue 30-year bonds, the tax subsidy would cost around $250 billion. However, a large fraction of the costs will be offset by the fact that new state workers would be in Social Security. According to estimates by Diamond and Orszag (2005), if all newly hired state and local government workers were on Social Security, it would eliminate 10 percent of the program's 75-year actuarial deficit, which today stands at $5.3 trillion. A little over two-thirds of state and local workers are on state-sponsored DB pension plans, so bringing these workers into Social Security would save 7 percent of that deficit, or $370 billion. If guarantees by the state to bring new workers into Social Security are only valid for half of the 75 years, the savings from the Social Security expansion would still be over $175 billion. These savings would be borne to some extent by state governments and future state employees paying into Social Security.

Including these gains to the Social Security system, the net cost to the federal government of the entire stabilization program would be only $75 billion. It would prevent a trillion-dollar crisis in less than a decade.

What about the cash flow of the states themselves? Social Security costs 12.4 percent of pay, divided equally among employer and employee. A typical DC plan costs a total of around 9 percent of pay (Poterba, Rauh, Venti, and Wise 2007). Total costs would therefore be 21.4 percent of pay. As a comparison, the plans offered to California state employees cost anywhere between 21.6 percent of pay for the least expensive workers to 40.1 percent of pay for the Highway Patrol Plan. Our proposal would allow states to borrow to meet their share of those costs for existing workers while establishing more sustainable systems for new workers. States would be paying DC contributions and the Social Security share only for new workers, so initially those cash flows would in fact be quite small, given that new hires are a small proportion of the workforce each year.

It is important to take measures that prevent the incoming revenue from new workers into Social Security from crowding out other adjustments that the federal government would otherwise have made to Social Security. Separate accounting should be made of the contributions from new state workers in order to discourage the federal government from raiding this pile of money to avoid other fixes it could have made to the program.

SECURE EXISTING PROMISES AND STOP UNFUNDED LIABILITIES

This plan offers substantial benefits to numerous parties. Specifically, pension promises made by states to their existing workers become more secure, since the funding of these obligations will greatly improve. New state workers get a retirement plan that is more than an empty promise. Taxpayers avoid massive future tax increases and loss of public services. And, critically, state politicians will no longer be able to use pensions as a vehicle for borrowing off the books at horizons that extend beyond their political careers.

While DC pension plans have some drawbacks, they are immune to the key accounting and accountability issues that have brought many states to the brink of insolvency. States and their employees have for decades been operating under a pretense that promised pension benefits do not represent a real cost, since they will not have to be met for many years. Our plan shifts $75 billion of pension costs for existing workers onto the federal government, but it would prevent a much larger future bailout.

It is instructive to compare our solution to a more extreme idea of waiting until funds run dry and then attempting to cut benefits. This approach would lead to shutdowns of state governments while legal battles are waged over employee rights. Many attempts to cut benefits would fail. Constitutional protections are strong in some of the more troubled states. Municipal bankruptcies such as Orange County in 1994 and the ongoing situation in Vallejo have shown that it is very difficult to cut pension benefits—even when bondholders and trade creditors are being impaired.

Some might argue that the federal government should simply take a hard line and announce that it will not, under any circumstance, help states with their pension problems. This approach suffers from the classic problem of time inconsistency. The inability to make credible commitments against bailouts made it impossible for the U.S. government to refuse to bail out large banks. There isn't even a bankruptcy procedure in place for failing states to restructure their debts, as there is for corporations (Chapter 11) or municipalities (Chapter 9).

Indeed, the federal government would almost certainly come to the rescue rather than watching a state fail. It is therefore imperative that we act today by giving states incentives to put themselves back on a path to fiscal sustainability.

REFERENCES AND FURTHER READING

Diamond, Peter A., and Peter R. Orszag. 2005. "Saving Social Security: The Diamond-Orszag Plan." *The Economists' Voice* 2, no. 1: art. 8. Available at www.bepress.com/ev/vol2/iss1/art8.

Poterba, James, Joshua Rauh, Steven Venti, and David Wise. 2007. "Defined Contribution Plans, Defined Benefit Plans, and the Accumulation of Retirement Wealth." *Journal of Public Economics* 91, no. 10: 2062–86. Available at http://econ-www.mit.edu/files/428.

Rauh, Joshua. 2010. "Are State Public Pensions Sustainable? Why the Federal Government Should Worry About State Pension Liabilities." *National Tax Journal*, May 15. Available at http://ssrn.com/abstract =1596679.

CHAPTER 27

Carbon Taxes to Move Toward Fiscal Sustainability

William D. Nordhaus

ALONG WITH MOST other high-income countries, the United States faces a major increase in the government debt relative to GDP. The most recent report of the Congressional Budget Office (CBO) in June 2010 estimated that the debt-GDP ratio will be between 65 and 72 percent in 2015 under alternative assumptions about the baseline fiscal policy. The debt ratio is increasing rapidly as a result of the collapse of revenues in the current extended downturn. In order to address this issue, the federal government has established the National Commission on Fiscal Responsibility and Reform. This group has been charged with "identifying policies to improve the fiscal situation in the medium term and to achieve fiscal sustainability over the long run."

The Commission has heard many proposals for increases in revenues. Most involve standard sources such as income, consumption, or company taxes. I would like to discuss a different focus, which is

William D. Nordhaus is Sterling Professor of Economics at Yale University.

the use of environmental taxes. I will concentrate here on the fiscal and economic advantages of a carbon tax.

A ONE-HANDED PROPOSAL

Harry Truman is reported to have complained that he didn't know a one-handed economist. His advisers were always saying, "On the one hand, on the other hand." This is a one-handed proposal for a carbon tax. Simply put, there is no better fiscal instrument to employ at this time, in this country, and given the fiscal constraints faced by the United States.

A carbon tax is a levy on emissions of carbon dioxide into the atmosphere; the term *carbon tax* is shorthand for a carbon dioxide tax, or CO_2 tax. The major source of carbon dioxide is the combustion of fossil fuels. The most efficient way to levy a carbon tax is on the carbon content of fossil fuels at the point of first sale or purchase. There should be no exemptions. I propose a schedule for the carbon tax rate later.

The desirable features of any tax are that it raises revenues in a manner that has minimal distortionary effect on the economy and reinforces other objectives of national policy. The following are the major reasons that a carbon tax meets these objectives. I will provide these in a summary form. The background literature provided at the end of this chapter explains these in greater detail.

- A carbon tax can raise a substantial amount of revenue over the coming decades.
- It is an instrument that has been used in other countries and is well understood.
- It is virtually the only tax under consideration that will increase economic efficiency because it reduces the output of an undesirable activity (carbon dioxide emissions). Every other tax that is under discussion will reduce economic efficiency.

- The carbon tax will move a long way toward implementing Congress's goals for climate change policy. The necessary condition for slowing climate change is to increase the price of carbon emissions. The carbon tax does this in a straightforward and transparent manner.
- A carbon tax will help meet international commitments that the United States has undertaken to reduce its carbon dioxide and other greenhouse gas emissions.
- A carbon tax will have substantial public health benefits because it will reduce harmful emissions, particularly those associated with burning coal.
- A carbon tax can buttress or replace many inefficient regulatory initiatives and will thereby provide yet another improvement in economic efficiency.
- A carbon tax could supplement or replace the cap-and-trade approach to limiting emissions. From a fiscal point of view, it has the distinct advantage of scooping up the "rents" that would accrue to those who receive free allocations of emissions permits under that plan.

Recent studies in economics have estimated the carbon tax that would be necessary to balance the economic costs of reducing carbon dioxide emissions with the gains in reducing the damages from climate change. The optimal carbon tax rises over time in real terms because damages rise with higher temperatures and a larger economy. Depending on the model and the objective, the optimal global carbon tax in current prices in 2015 would be between $12 and $25 per ton of carbon dioxide. The appropriate tax should rise about 6 percent per year in real or inflation-corrected terms to reflect the increasing cost of future emissions.

This level of tax would be justified purely on environmental grounds. There is no formula that would tell how much might be added for purposes of raising revenues, but my judgment is that the upper end of the range just cited would serve a good balance of environmental and macroeconomic objectives. A reasonable approach would be a carbon tax in 2015 of $25 per ton of carbon dioxide equivalent, levied on all sources of carbon dioxide emissions. This would be phased in as the economy returns to full employment.

To understand how a carbon tax would look on the ground, consider the prices of electricity and gasoline as examples. The average U.S. household consumes about 12,000 kilowatt hours (kWhs) of electricity per year at an average price of about $0.10 per kWh. If this electricity is generated from coal, that would lead to about 12 tons of carbon dioxide emissions. If the carbon price were $25 per ton of carbon dioxide, this would increase the annual cost of 12,000 kWhs of coal-electricity purchases from $1,200 to $1,500. By contrast, the costs of nuclear or wind power would be unaffected by a carbon tax because they use essentially no carbon fuels.

Most people are surprised to learn that the effect on gasoline prices is relatively small. The $25 carbon tax would raise gasoline prices only 25 cents a gallon. The reason for the difference between coal-electricity and gasoline is that the former has a high carbon content per dollar of expenditure, while the latter has relatively little.

POINTS OF INTERPRETATION

I add several points of interpretation and practicality.

First, the carbon tax has the advantage that its optimal structure is back-loaded. That is, the optimal environmental tax rate rises over time, and the revenues also therefore rise rapidly over time. This is particularly helpful in the current macroeconomic situation because it would not be wise to introduce a sharp increase in taxes while the economy is mired in a deep recession.

Second, the United States should work with other countries so that all major countries can introduce an internationally harmonized tax on carbon dioxide emissions. Such an approach will maximize the environmental benefits in curbing global warming and reduce the dangers of triggering trade wars revolving around different global warming policies.

Third, the issue of how rapidly to introduce the tax is an important one. A carbon tax has a relatively narrow base and would have a major impact on carbon-intensive industries. For this reason, it would be wise to phase in the tax gradually, perhaps over a five-year period. A gradual introduction is far preferable to the alternative of providing exemptions to the heavily affected industries. A low but universal tax is more efficient than a high but narrow tax.

Fourth, there will be concerns that a carbon tax will damage the economy. We should always ask, "Compared to what?" The advantage of a carbon tax along the lines sketched here is that it improves the long-run sustainability of both the fiscal system and the environment relative to other options.

Fifth, there is no doubt that a carbon tax will disadvantage particular sectors or firms—those that are in highly carbon-intensive sectors. But it must be emphasized that the whole purpose of a carbon tax is to reduce the output of products that are carbon-intensive. Prices must rise in these sectors to ensure that consumers change their consumption patterns and that firms choose low-carbon technologies or invent new ones. There may be cases where severe hardships will occur, such as for coal miners. In this case, it would be useful to craft transitional measures that will help workers and communities adapt to a world of high carbon prices rather than to shield them from the high prices and delay the transition.

Sixth, from an environmental point of view, it is necessary that the tax be stable, consistent, predictable, and durable. It should be a fiscal structure that the United States is committed to, so that businesses can rely upon it for long-term planning purposes. This is particularly important for electric utilities and other very large long-term capital projects.

Finally, should we be concerned about the regressivity of a carbon tax? Again, we must ask, compared to what? Existing research on this topic suggests that it has approximately the same distributional impact as a value-added tax or as the current payroll tax associated with Social Security. It has the same impact on energy prices as a cap-and-trade plan, but it allows the government to capture the revenues. A carbon tax is likely to be much less regressive than the impacts of global warming. Note as well that conspicuous consumption in gas-guzzling private jets, mega-yachts, and first-class travel will be subject to a big carbon-tax levy.

IMPLICATIONS FOR REVENUES AND THE FEDERAL DEBT

A carbon tax can produce substantial revenues in the coming years. Based on my emissions projections, the recommended carbon tax would yield $134 billion of current revenues in 2015, equal to about 0.6 percent of GDP. The calculations are shown in Table 27.1.

TABLE 27.1

Projected Carbon Tax Revenues

Year	Tax rate ($/ton CO_2)	Emissions (billions, tons CO_2)	Revenues (billions, current $)	Revenues (percent of GDP)
2005	0.0	6.1	0	0.00
2015	25.0	4.9	123	0.63
2020	39.7	4.6	184	0.74
2025	63.0	4.5	282	0.91
2030	89.8	4.3	386	1.00
2035	128.1	4.1	528	1.09

Assumptions

1. Inflation at 2.5 percent per year
2. Long-term real GDP growth at 2.5 percent per year

Because the tax rate is rising sharply, the revenues would also increase substantially over time.

Recall the charge to the fiscal commission to improve the fiscal situation in the medium term and to achieve fiscal sustainability over the long run. Some have focused on the short-term objective of targets for the federal deficit in 2015. While specific flow or deficit targets are useful guidelines, the ultimate target is to reduce the trend of net federal debt. This is best measured by the impact of a proposal on the net present value of taxes or spending.

We can appraise the carbon tax in terms of its impact on the net debt. The CBO, in its last full report in June 2010, projected that the baseline net government debt at the end of FY 2015 will be between 65 and 72 percent of GDP, depending upon the scenario (extended baseline and alternative fiscal, respectively). The present value of tax revenues from the carbon-tax proposal presented here is 15 percent of GDP through 2030 and 35 percent of GDP through 2050. (These are calculated at a nominal discount rate of 5 percent per year, which is the CBO estimate of the long-term government-borrowing rate.) Over the medium term to 2050, then, a carbon tax can make a substantial contribution to fiscal balance.

REFERENCES AND FURTHER READING

Congressional Budget Office. 2010. *The Long Term Budget Outlook,* June. Available at www.cbo.gov/ftpdocs/88xx/doc8877/12–13-LTBO.pdf.

Metcalf, Gilbert E., and David Weisbach. 2009. "The Design of a Carbon Tax." *Harvard Environmental Law Review* 33. Available at www.law .harvard.edu/students/orgs/elr/vol33_2/Metcalf%20Weisbach.pdf.

Nordhaus, William. 2008. *A Question of Balance: Weighing the Options on Global Warming Policies.* New Haven, Conn.: Yale University Press. Available at http://yalepress.yale.edu/book.asp?isbn=9780300137484.

Nordhaus, William. 2010. "Economic Aspects of Global Warming in a Post-Copenhagen Environment." Proceedings of the National Academy of Sciences (U.S.). Available at www.pnas.org/content/early/2010 /06/10/1005985107.

CHAPTER 28

Net Neutrality Is Bad Broadband Regulation

Robert E. Litan and Hal J. Singer

AMERICA NEEDS JOBS, and President Obama is facing a serious problem of how to get them. Private-sector job creation in 2010 has been a paltry 100,000 per month. At that pace, it would take over three years to restore just the nearly four million private-sector jobs lost in the first six months of 2009, let alone absorb new and discouraged workers coming into the labor force.

Jobs require private investment. After all, there is little appetite in Washington or among the public generally for additional federal stimulus. Moreover, there are few, if any, macroeconomic "bullets"

Robert E. Litan is Vice President for Research and Policy at the Kauffman Foundation in Kansas City, a Senior Fellow in Economic Studies at the Brookings Institution, and a Senior Consultant with Navigant Economics. He has served in a number of federal government positions, including Deputy Assistant Attorney General in the Justice Department's Antitrust Division (1993–1995). Hal J. Singer is a Managing Director at Navigant Economics and has served as Adjunct Professor at the McDonough School of Business at Georgetown University. The views expressed here are those of the authors and should not be attributed to their employers. The authors have consulted for telecommunications companies in regulatory proceedings.

left at the Federal Reserve, which already has greatly expanded the money supply and reduced short-term interest rates to near zero.

However, private capital is waiting on the sidelines. America's 500 largest nonfinancial companies have stashed away nearly $1.8 trillion of cash on their balance sheets according to Federal Reserve statistics.[1] If the administration could get these funds to flow into the economy, the recovery would ramp up into high gear.

Why the trepidation among investors? The overriding reason is weak consumer demand and fears that this will continue. A contributing factor, however, is that businesses are uncertain about the government's appetite for further regulation. Experience shows that in order to preserve private-sector incentives to invest, especially in a capital-intensive industry like telecom, policy makers should intervene only to correct a market failure. Even then, policy makers should weigh the benefits and costs of new regulation on consumer welfare (a short-run concern) and on investment incentives (a long-run concern).

NET NEUTRALITY AND INVESTMENT INCENTIVES

The administration's evolving policies in the telecom arena do not meet these criteria. The Federal Communications Commission (FCC) has set in motion a rule-making proceeding designed to make "net neutrality" a permanent part of the regulatory landscape. To do so, the FCC is seeking to reclassify Internet service providers (ISPs)—from a light-touch "Title I" to a heavy-handed "Title II" designation.

Title II rules were designed to rein in monopoly telephone carriers of the twentieth century, which could not be counted on to price their services at competitive levels. But are such rules needed for broadband? Except in the most remote areas, consumers have a choice of at least three types of broadband providers: cable, DSL (digital subscriber line), and wireless. No monopoly here.

Recognizing that there is no broadband monopoly and that heavy-handed regulation could freeze broadband investment in its tracks, the FCC is promising that the current and *future* FCC would refrain from invoking the more draconian levers available under Title II, including price regulation. But can telecoms rely on this promise?

The verdict from the markets is "no." Investment analysts, for example, have noted that the major telecom carriers are already paying significant dividends—even more than tobacco companies—suggesting that they are too worried about future regulation to invest this money. One economic study by the Phoenix Center estimates that the May 6, 2010, announcement of the FCC's plans to reclassify Internet service shaved 10 percent from the value of stocks of cable companies that also would be subject to the FCC's proposed new Title II regulatory regime (controlling for movements in the broader stock index) but had no effect on the stock prices of direct broadcast satellite providers that would not be subject to the proposed reclassi-fication. In short, the markets are telling policy makers that the proposed regulatory shift is *already* adversely affecting investment prospects in the telecoms sector and blocking the jobs that such investment could generate.

To understand why the telecoms and their current and future shareholders are spooked, one must understand the meaning of net neutrality. Net neutrality has come to mean that all content providers pay the same price and have the same access to final consumers. Advocates have the understandable goal of ensuring that ISPs do not advantage one content provider over another. But instead of the widely accepted and proven non-discrimination provisions in other areas of communications (such as cable programming), which provide independent programmers a forum to adjudicate their "program carriage" complaints, the FCC has crafted a brand-new concept of non-discrimination solely for the Internet that can only harm future investment and reduce consumer welfare. As laid out by the Commission, nondiscrimination (i.e., "net neutrality") under the FCC's proposal means that ISPs cannot offer enhanced services to content providers *at any price except zero*. That some content providers may not afford priority service at a positive price does not constitute discrimination; there are many upgrades in life—from navigation systems on cars to private lounges in airports—that are not free.

Why do we worry about this policy? Enhanced connectivity would enable real-time applications to operate free of jitter and perform at higher levels. And, competitive pressure would force ISPs to use at least some of the money raised from these enhancements to lower the price of broadband access to end users. Unfortunately, as long as ISPs are barred from charging for enhanced services, they won't offer them.

There is no getting around the fact that telling a firm that it can't charge for a service is price regulation, notwithstanding the Commission's claims to the contrary. Like with any regulation, if the regulator sets the wrong price, problems emerge. Setting a price of zero for valuable enhancements is quite simply the wrong price.

LESSONS FROM TWO-SIDED MARKETS

The prospect of future price regulation of ISPs is of more than academic interest. It is well established that price regulation often truncates the returns on an investment in a regulated industry, and thereby decreases investment. Likewise, net neutrality would reduce the profitability of broadband networks, and thus discourage network investment by ISPs.

To see why, consider two regulatory regimes: one in which an ISP may charge content providers for enhanced services, and another in which such charges are prohibited (net neutrality regulation). Even according to a theoretical model championed by net neutrality proponents, end users are unequivocally worse off under net neutrality regulation, as the end-user price of broadband access is *always higher* when ISPs are barred from raising revenues from content providers. This is the seesaw principle in action—placing downward pressure on price on one side of the market (for content providers) leads to upward pressure on price on the other side of the market (for end users), as described by economists Jean-Charles Rochet and Jean Tirole (2006).

For those who are skeptical about this result, think what would happen if newspapers, another two-sided platform, were suddenly restrained from charging advertisers for ads. The daily price of a newspaper would rise.

Because end users are more sensitive to price increases than are content providers, the incremental revenues raised on end users under a net neutrality regime cannot compensate ISPs for the foregone revenues on content providers; that means that the profitability of the broadband network will decline under a price-regulated net neutrality regime. Lower profitability means lower returns, which in turn means less investment.

To be sure, some content providers that would otherwise pay ISPs for enhanced services might benefit from net neutrality rules, which is no doubt the main reason they vigorously advocate such rules. But the *absence* of net neutrality regulation won't necessarily reduce investment by content providers, and it might even increase their investment.

Suppose, for example, that an ISP offered special handling of a content provider's data packets for $1,000 per month. Content providers with no need for such enhancements would simply decline the offer. No investment risk there. Now consider content providers who can make use of the enhanced services. Those content providers might invest more (relative to a net neutrality regime) in developing applications that take advantage of the new feature.

Setting aside the welfare of end users (which is always lower under net neutrality rules), policy makers must balance the investment risk faced by ISPs in the *presence* of net neutrality rules against the (however implausible) investment risk faced by content providers in the *absence* of net neutrality rules. ISPs are set to invest $30 billion annually over the next five years to blanket the country with next-generation broadband networks, nearly half of which ($14 billion per year) will support wireless networks, according to Robert Atkinson and Ivy Schultz (2009) of the Columbia Institute for Tele-Information. That's a lot of investment at risk.

It is difficult to estimate with precision what portion of the $30 billion would be eliminated in the presence of net neutrality rules, but the direction of the impact—negative—is clear. One paper by Cambridge Strategic Management Group (2009) estimates that the FCC's planned reclassification of ISPs would cause 47 percent fewer households to financially justify fiber-to-the-home investment, impacting some 29 million homes nationwide. Noted telecom analyst Craig Moffett of Bernstein Research opines that, with the imposition of net neutrality rules and Title II reclassification, Verizon FiOS "would be stopped in its tracks," AT&T's U-Verse "deployments would slow," and Clearwire's investment in wireless 4G service might be scaled back. Bank of America/Merrill Lynch and Standard and Poor's reached similar conclusions regarding adverse investment effects.[2]

And on the other side of the ledger? Crickets.

We are not aware of any study that purports to estimate the aggregate investment by content providers over the coming years or the alleged increase in aggregate investment by content providers owing to net neutrality regulation. Absent such data, it is irresponsible for government policy makers to move forward with the proposed system of net neutrality regulation.

Because content providers are agitating for government intervention, they should bear the burden of demonstrating that *aggregate* investment across the "edge" and "core" of the network would not decline under their exotic strand of nondiscrimination. In other words, they must show that the increase in content provider investment under a net neutrality regime will more than offset the decrease in ISP investment. Today there is no such proof, and we doubt they can make the case.

A BETTER WAY FORWARD

So if net neutrality regulation is bad policy, what should the Commission be doing to encourage investment by *both* Internet providers and content providers?

We concede that independent content providers need assurance that they will not be discriminated against when it comes to accessing broadband subscribers or buying enhanced quality of service from ISPs (this is a very different thing from paying nothing for enhanced service under net neutrality). The best way to do this is to "use the basic principles animating antitrust law to fill in the content of the case-by-case analysis," as explained by Professor Christopher Yoo (2009) of the University of Pennsylvania Law School.

In fact, the FCC already uses a case-by-case process to adjudicate discrimination complaints brought by independent cable networks against vertically integrated cable operators. Why should the FCC use one process to adjudicate discrimination claims in the Internet space and a different process in the cable programming space? The recent *WealthTV* and *NFL Network* court cases made clear that the process is not stacked in favor of complainants, but the process does properly place the burden squarely on the complainant to prove that (1) it has been discriminated against on the basis of affiliation and (2) as a result of that discrimination, the complainant has been materially impaired in its ability to compete against the affiliated provider. Importing that framework here, a disgruntled content provider should be required to make the same showing to the FCC.

Such a process would leave ISPs free to contract—at a positive price—with content providers for enhanced services offerings. Although the importation of the current dispute-resolution process from the cable programming space to the Internet space might require new legislation, that is not a bad thing; the regulatory agenda should flow from Congress to the Commission.

These two policies—assurance that ISPs' investments will not be appropriated and that independent content providers will not be anti-competitively discriminated against—would create an ideal investment climate for ISPs and for content providers. Such an outcome is critical because it can help boost the economy in general by opening the door to telecommunications investment and job creation.

NOTES

1. Federal Reserve, "Nonfarm Nonfinancial Corporate Business Total Liquid Assets, Flow of Funds." Available at www.federalreserve .gov/releases/z1/current/accessible/l102.htm.
2. Bank of America/Merrill Lynch, "Internet Regulation Back on the Front Burner," May 5, 2010; W. Spain, "FCC Chief Broaches New Approach on 'Net Neutrality,'" *MarketWatch,* May 6, 2010.

REFERENCES AND FURTHER READING

Atkinson, Robert C., and Ivy E. Schultz. 2009. "Broadband in America: Where It Is and Where It Is Going (According to Broadband Service Providers)." Columbia Institute for Tele-Information. November 11. Table 15. Available at www.broadband.gov/docs/Broadband_in _America.pdf.

Bank of America/Merrill Lynch. 2010. "Internet Regulation Back on the Front Burner." May 5.

Cambridge Strategic Management Group. 2009. "National Broadband Plan Policy Evaluation." November 2. Prepared for Fiber to the Home Council. Available at www.ftthcouncil.org/node/723.

Economides, Nicholas, and Joachim Tåg. 2007. "Net Neutrality on the Internet: A Two-Sided Market Analysis." NET Institute Working

Paper No. 07–45. Available at www.stern.nyu.edu/networks/Econo mides_Tag_Net_Neutrality.pdf.

Hank, Robert, Robert Litan, and Hal Singer. 2010. "Addressing the Next Wave of Internet Regulation: Toward a Workable Principle for Nondiscrimination." *Regulation & Governance.*

Phoenix Center. 2010. "The Broadband Credibility Gap." June. Available at www.phoenix-center.org/pcpp/PCPP40Final.pdf.

Rochet, Jean-Charles, and Jean Tirole. 2006. "Two-Sided Markets: A Progress Report." *RAND Journal of Economics* 37, no. 3. Available at www.jstor.org/pss/25046265.

Spain, W. 2010. "FCC Chief Broaches New Approach on 'Net Neutrality.'" *MarketWatch,* May 6. Available at www.marketwatch.com/story /cable-shares-hit-by-fcc-move-on-netneutrality-2010–05–06.

Yoo, Christopher. 2009. "Network Neutrality After Comcast: Toward a Case-by-Case Approach to Reasonable Network Management." University of Pennsylvania Law School Research Paper No. 09–36. Available at http://papers.ssrn.com/sol3/papers.cfm?abstract_id=1511892.

CHAPTER 29

Trills Instead of T-Bills: It's Time to Replace Part of Government Debt with Shares in GDP

Mark J. Kamstra and Robert J. Shiller

AT THIS TIME of intense national debate on the rapidly rising national debt and on fundamental financial reform, a time of unusual economic and financial uncertainty, it is vitally important to reconsider the structure of government obligations. We believe that, in parallel with the many other ongoing changes in our financial structure, the obligations of the national government should take a new and innovative form.

Consider a new U.S. government-issued security, with a coupon tied to the United States' gross domestic product (GDP) in current dollars. Ideally, this security would be long term in maturity, perhaps even perpetual.

Mark J. Kamstra is an Associate Professor of Finance at the Schulich School of Business, York University. Robert J. Shiller is the Arthur M. Okun Professor of Economics, Professor of Finance at the Department of Economics and School of Management, Yale University, Research Associate, National Bureau of Economic Research, and Chief Economist, MacroMarkets LLC.

We propose a small-denomination GDP share paying a coupon each year of one-trillionth of that year's GDP, or about $14.60 at current levels. On this basis, we suggest the name "Trill" be used to refer to this new security. Similar to shares issued by corporations paying a fraction of corporate earnings in dividends, the Trill would pay a fraction of the "earnings" of the United States.

The capital structure of the U.S. government, as with other countries, is entirely tilted to fixed-income debt obligations (similar to corporate debt) with nothing analogous to the equity funding available to corporations. That means that the residual claimant on government operations is the domestic taxpayer, coerced into playing this risky role, instead of willing investors, as is the case with corporate equity. As the national debt rises, the implicit leverage borne by the taxpayer is rising. We believe that investors would be enthusiastic to bear some of this risk.

Currently, investors can purchase a fairly comprehensive menu of assets with which to diversify a portfolio. In spite of their scope, however, these securities represent a small fraction of the wealth of the nation. Roughly two-thirds of the U.S. GDP is made up of wages, salaries, and supplementary labor income, but trading on claims to these income flows is for all intents and purposes unavailable to markets and investors. In the language of financial economists, the current menu of available assets is *incomplete*. There are risks in the economy, related specifically to human capital and the GDP, that cannot be traded in existing financial markets, and this results in the underdiversification of many, if not all, investors and certainly pensioners with no wage income.

The implicit portfolio of the U.S. government is long on claims to labor income (as well as corporate earnings) and short fixed incomes. Good times or bad, payments must be made on fixed-coupon government debt, and in deep recessions, countries, like companies, can have cash inflows and outflows so badly matched that financing crises occur.

Trills would have coupon payments that would rise in an expansion, be of value to investors, and, importantly, for the U.S. government would decline in a recession with declining tax revenues, in contrast to existing debt vehicles.

From a Keynesian stabilization perspective, the higher interest payments in better times may seem unfortunately procyclical. But, again from that perspective, payments of interest on the national debt are not quickly spent by consumers, having a low multiplier. In practice, the new securities would relieve recessionary pressures on the government so that it could better conduct effective stabilizing stimuli.

From the perspective of the U.S. government, such a new security would diversify obligations. Risk-sharing with the private sector can improve the risk-return trade-off of investors, the classic win-win through financial innovation and diversification.

HISTORY OF GDP SECURITIES

To the best of our knowledge, true GDP shares have not yet been issued by any country. One of us (Shiller) proposed GDP shares in a 1993 book, but no such shares were issued; others have made analogous proposals.

By the mid-1990s bonds with attached GDP warrants were issued by Bulgaria, Bosnia, and Costa Rica in concert with their Brady Plan restructurings. These bonds included clauses to increase coupon payments at predetermined GDP thresholds rather than in lockstep with the GDP and were not designed well enough to bring on a groundswell of investor interest.

In contrast, the Trill would be as simple and familiar as shares in corporations. We believe that transparency and simple structure are essential to establishing demand for these securities and ensuring that their market is liquid.

Our partial-equilibrium analysis suggests that the cost of issuance of the Trill may be in the order of 150 basis points above short-term government debt. The government should be willing to pay this extra return on behalf of taxpayers, since it helps it manage risks.

The costs may be different if we admit some general equilibrium considerations (see Athanasoulis and Shiller 2001). In Athanasoulis and Shiller's model, introducing Trill-like securities would raise the riskless rate of interest in the new general equilibrium and raise the discount rate for risky assets. The higher riskless rate is unambiguously welfare improving in this model.

The model is only suggestive for the real world, since it relies on some narrow assumptions. But if there is a higher riskless rate after Trills, it should be thought of as a symptom of better investment opportunities for the people and reduced exposure to tax risk, not higher government borrowing costs.

The dividend yield on Trills is likely to be extremely low now, since investors are likely to expect real GDP to grow at something like its historical rate of over 3 percent a year. The low dividend yield will reduce the immediate cash-flow problem of the government.

WHY INVESTORS NEED TRILLS

Of particular note in light of recent market turmoil, Trills would have virtually no counterparty risk, in contrast to currently available assets that protect relative standards of living in retirement. Because nominal GDP would be used to determine a Trill's coupon value, the inflation-protection properties of the Trill would resemble those of the U.S. Treasury's Inflation-Protected Securities (TIPS). Inflation protection alone would be sufficient to generate interest in Trills comparable to that which exists for TIPS. Further interest would be generated since Trills would protect relative standards of living in retirement, as they are a constant share of GDP, in contrast to TIPS, which purchase a declining real share of a growing GDP over time.

Creation of Trills can be motivated in terms of models of intergenerational risk-sharing. There is a small literature that considers the benefits of intergenerational risk-smoothing through long-lived assets. Some of this work does not involve government debt (as argued by Dan Peled 1984; Franklin Allen and David Gale 1997; and John Geanakoplos 2008), though much of this literature does investigate the impact of government debt on welfare. Gale (1990) shows that uncertainty in an overlapping generations (OLG) model leads to incompleteness and allows for government debt issuance to be Pareto-improving through its impact on intergenerational transfers.

Improvements in welfare may not be surprising with incomplete markets. In this case the government can provide innovative financial securities and complete markets. Even if markets are complete, however, in an OLG model the competitive equilibrium may be inefficient so that government debt or transfers can still improve welfare, as Gabrielle Demange (2002) has shown.

Henning Bohn (1990) has made a strong argument for government liabilities that provides a hedge (for the government) against macroeconomic shocks to smooth tax revenues and maximize welfare. He finds that shorting the stock market is one way this could be accomplished. Of course, issuance of Trills is a more natural way for the government to do this. Bohn (1999, 2001) builds on a model of Diamond (1965) to show that in an OLG neoclassical framework, government use of debt is potentially welfare improving because of inefficiencies in the allocation of risk across generations, in particular the problem that future (unborn) generations are naturally excluded from financial markets.

Dirk Kruger and Felix Kubler (2006) applied Paul Samuelson's overlapping generations model to show that government interventions analogous to Trills can be Pareto-improving. Trills can also be motivated in terms of models of international risk-sharing, as described by Stefano Athanasoulis, Robert Shiller, and Eric van Wincoop (1999).

As we detailed in 2009, we can, subject to some assumptions, estimate the return in the future to holding a Trill. Standard mean-variance (return versus risk) optimization over asset classes, including the estimated return to holding Trills, suggests that Trills might allow investors a return very nearly as high as the S&P 500, with half the volatility. Indeed, investors gain a much higher return and lower volatility than if Trills are excluded from the mix. This mean-variance optimization produces an optimal portfolio composition of 28 percent of assets in long-term bonds, 38 percent in the S&P 500 index, and 34 percent in Trills. Thus the addition of Trills to the asset mix available today would likely have a dramatic impact on investor portfolio composition and investor well-being.

It may go without saying, but Trills should never replace conventional government debt completely. Capital markets rely on the term structure of U.S. government nominal debt as a reference point for pricing other fixed-coupon nominal debt, and as a hedging instrument.

THE URGENCY

Public confidence may be boosted if the U.S. government does something fundamental to correct the faulty risk management implicit in pure-debt government financing that helped make the current crisis as bad as it is, and that inhibits a constructive response to the crisis.

Despite rising concerns about U.S. government solvency, U.S. government bonds currently remain in high demand, and thus their market yield is low. We suspect that the same remarkable demand, even more remarkable perhaps, may extend to Trills.

REFERENCES AND FURTHER READING

Allen, Franklin, and David Gale. 1997. "Financial Markets, Intermediaries, and Intertemporal Smoothing." *Journal of Political Economy* 105, no. 3: 523–46. Available at http://papers.ssrn.com/sol3/papers.cfm?abstract_id=8633.

Athanasoulis, Stefano, and Robert J. Shiller. 2001. "World Income Components: Measuring and Exploiting International Risk Sharing Opportunities." *American Economic Review* 91, no. 4: 1031–54. Available at www.nber.org/papers/w5095.

Athanasoulis, Stefano, Robert J. Shiller, and Eric van Wincoop. 1999. "Macro Markets and Financial Security." *Economic Policy Review* 5, no. 1: 21–39. Available at www.newyorkfed.org/research/epr/99v05n1/9904atha.pdf.

Bohn, Henning. 1990. "Tax Smoothing with Financial Instruments." *American Economic Review* 80, no. 5: 1217–30. Available at www.jstor.org/pss/2006771.

Bohn, Henning. 1999. "Should the Social Security Trust Fund Hold Equities? An Intergenerational Welfare Analysis." *Review of Economic Dynamics* 2: 666–97. Available at http://econpapers.repec.org/paper/redappend/bohn99.htm.

Bohn, Henning. 2001. "Social Security and Demographic Uncertainty: The Risk Sharing Properties of Alternative Policies." In *Risk Aspects of Investment-Based Social Security Reform,* ed. John Campbell and Martin Feldstein, 203–41. Chicago, Ill.: University of Chicago Press.

Demange, Gabrielle. 2002. "On Optimality in Intergenerational Risk Sharing." *Economic Theory* 20: 1–27. Available at www.jstor.org/pss/25055510.

Diamond, Peter. 1965. "National Debt in a Neoclassical Growth Model." *American Economic Review* 55: 1126–50. Available at www.jstor.org/stable/1809231.

Gale, Douglas. 1990. "The Efficient Design of Public Debt." In *Public Debt Management: Theory and History,* ed. R. Dornbusch and M. Draghi, 14–51. Cambridge: Cambridge University Press.

Geanakoplos, John. 2008. "Overlapping Generations Models of General Equilibrium." Yale University, Cowles Foundation Discussion Paper No. 1663, May. Available at http://cowles.econ.yale.edu/P/cd/d16b/d1663.pdf.

Jacobius, Arleen. 2009. "Funds Pour Big Money Into Realm of Real Assets." *Pensions and Investments,* January 26. Available at www.pionline.com/article20090126/PRINTSUB/901239991.

Kamstra, Mark J., and Robert J. Shiller. 2008. "The Case for Trills: Giving Canadians and Their Pension Funds a Stake in the Wealth of the Nation." C. D. Howe Institute Commentary, *The Pension Papers* 271 (August). Available at http://econpapers.repec.org/article/cdhcommen/271.htm.

Kamstra, Mark J., and Robert J. Shiller. 2009. "The Case for Trills: Giving the People and Their Pension Funds a Stake in the Wealth of the Nation." Yale University, Cowles Foundation Discussion Paper No. 1717. August. Available at http://cowles.econ.yale.edu/P/cd/d17a/d1717.pdf.

Kruger, Dirk, and Felix Kubler. 2006. "Pareto-Improving Social Security Reform When Financial Markets Are Incomplete." *The American Economic Review* 96, no. 3 (June): 737–55. Available at http://papers.ssrn.com/sol3/papers.cfm?abstract_id=774185.

Peled, Dan. 1984. "Stationary Pareto Optimality of Stochastic Asset Equilibria with Overlapping Generations." *Journal of Economic Theory* 34: 396–403. Available at http://linkinghub.elsevier.com/retrieve/pii/0022053184901546.

Samuelson, Paul A. 1958. "An Exact Consumption Loan Model of Interest with or Without the Social Contrivance of Money." *Journal of Political Economy* 66: 467–82. Available at www.jstor.org/pss/182698.

Shiller, Robert. 1993. *Macro Markets: Creating Institutions for Managing Society's Largest Economic Risks.* New York: Oxford University Press.

CHAPTER 30

The Google Book Settlement: Real Magic or a Trick?

Pamela Samuelson

PAUL COURANT (2009) has made a pragmatic argument in favor of the proposed settlement of the *Authors Guild v. Google* lawsuit that charged Google with copyright infringement for digitizing millions of books for its Google Book Search (GBS) initiative.

I agree with Courant that it is socially desirable for millions of out-of-print books in the collections of major research libraries, such as University of Michigan's, of which he is head librarian, to be digitized and made more widely accessible. And, indeed, the approval of the settlement would bring about greater access to these books.

Courant, like other proponents of the proposed settlement, which was announced in October of 2008, cast it as a win-win-win: for Google, the public, and rights holders who would stand to benefit from Google's commercialization of books in the GBS corpus if they

Pamela Samuelson is the Richard M. Sherman Distinguished Professor of Law and Information at the University of California, Berkeley, a world-renowned expert on copyright, and a past Fellow of the John D. and Catherine T. MacArthur Foundation.

signed up with the Google Partner Program, or a new collecting society, the Book Rights Registry (BRR), which would be established upon approval of the settlement. However, a closer examination of the terms of the proposed settlement casts the deal in a far different and more troubling light.

There are three main problems with the settlement. First, there are insufficient checks and balances in the settlement agreement to prevent abuses that seem likely to manifest themselves over time. Second, this settlement is deeply unfair to tens, if not hundreds, of thousands of members of the class on whose behalf the plaintiffs in the *Authors Guild* case purport to be acting. The third, which I won't address here, are the antitrust objections of the Department of Justice (DOJ) (for which Courant proposes a partial fix).

I DON'T BELIEVE IN MAGIC

Courant professes to be disinterested in legal process issues. At the "D is for Digitize" conference at New York Law School on October 9, 2009, he characterized the GBS class action settlement as "a magic trick." For Google to get a license to every in-copyright book on the planet for a mere $125 million—$45.5 million of which would go to the lawyers representing the author and publisher subclasses, and $34.5 million to fund the BRR's initial operations—by settling this lawsuit does seem like "magic." Google planned to set aside only $45 million to pay registered rights holders $60 each for scanning their in-copyright books. (Contrast this sum with the $1.65 billion Google paid to acquire YouTube, which at the time featured fewer than three million amateur videos.)

But the law is not magic, and magic is not the law. The GBS settlement contravenes core rule of law principles of our society. To accomplish such an extraordinarily comprehensive restructuring of the future market for digitized books requires legislative action. If the

GBS deal really was the complete win-win-win that its proponents believe, then it shouldn't be difficult for those who negotiated the deal to persuade Congress to bless it.

INSUFFICIENT CHECKS AND BALANCES

The most serious and widely shared concern expressed by academic author and library commentators on the GBS settlement is the risk that GBS institutional license fees will rise to exorbitant levels because the proposed settlement lacks meaningful constraints on price hikes.

The settlement agreement establishes four criteria for determining prices of institutional subscriptions: the number of books available, the quality of the scans, features offered as part of the subscription, and prices of similar products and services available from third parties. The more books Google scans and the more features it adds, the more justification it would have to raise prices. Google's chief spokesman for GBS, Dan Clancy, has publicly stated that there are no comparable products or services to the GBS institutional subscriptions, so this too will not serve as a check on price hikes. And it is doubtful that a similar product or service could ever be developed, because no other firm could realistically get a comparably broad (let alone, as inexpensive) license to in-copyright books as that which Google would get from the settling class.

Google founder Sergey Brin (2009) has said that "anyone can do what we did." This is misleading because GBS began as a scan-to-index project—for which there was, at least before this settlement, a plausible fair use defense—that has now morphed into a joint venture to sell books. The DOJ rejected the argument that "a competitor could enter the market by copying books en masse without permission in the hope of prompting a class action suit that could then be settled on terms comparable to the Proposed Settlement. Even if there were reasons to think that history could repeat itself in this unlikely fashion, it would scarcely be sound policy to encourage deliberate copyright violations and additional litigation as a means of obtaining approval for licensing provisions that could otherwise not be negotiated lawfully."[1]

Although institutional subscription prices might be quite modest initially in order to attract customers, my letter to the court on behalf of sixty-five academic authors expressed concern that "ten, twenty, thirty or more years from now, when institutions have become ever more dependent on GBS subscriptions and have consequently shed books from their physical collections, and indeed when electronic publishing begins to supplant traditional methods of publication for some texts, the temptation to raise prices to excessive levels will be very high."[2] Universities have suffered gravely from exorbitant price hikes of scholarly journals and bundling practices of for-profit publishers. Major library associations have told the court they perceive GBS subscriptions to pose similar risks.

Courant's recent essay downplayed the risk of price gouging. Yet he must once have believed that this risk was quite real, otherwise the University of Michigan would not have negotiated for an arbitration procedure to challenge excessive pricing in its May 2009 agreement with Google. This procedure, which can be invoked by any university library, not just by Michigan, is truly Byzantine, even Kafkaesque, in its complexity and limitations (e.g., there is no right to appeal). Yet even ignoring its opacity, the fundamental problem is that the settlement agreement contains no criteria for meaningful limitations on price hikes. It is, therefore, unlikely that the arbitration procedure in the Google–Michigan agreement will prove to be more than a symbolic gesture.

Courant agreed with me at the "D is for Digitize" conference that libraries would be over a barrel with Google insofar as they started shedding physical books from their collections as unneeded after a GBS subscription became available. Books take up a lot of valuable real estate in libraries, and they are also costly to maintain and process. So the temptation to get rid of books will be high once people take for granted that GBS is available.

Even if one believes that Google would not price gouge any time soon, it is important to realize that Google cannot set prices alone; it must do so in conjunction with the BRR, which would be dominated by trade publishers and professional writers who can be expected to press for ever higher prices.

Ten or twenty years from now, moreover, Google may lose interest in GBS and sell the corpus and its license to in-copyright books to the highest bidder. There is nothing in the settlement agreement to stop the highest bidder from raising prices to exorbitant levels. And presumably the only reason to bid on the corpus would be to extract more rents than Google had been doing. Nor does the agreement seem to preclude Google or its successor from shutting down the GBS service or destroying the GBS corpus. It would be tragic for this substantial public good to fall into the wrong hands or be destroyed.

The settlement agreement is also disturbingly silent about user privacy issues. It calls for lots of monitoring of individual uses of books but says nothing about what can or will be done with the data collected. Linguist Geoff Nunberg (2009) has characterized GBS as a "disaster for scholars" because its metadata (name of the book, the author, etc.) is pervasively erroneous. Also troubling is the right Google has to remove up to 15 percent of the books from the corpus for editorial or non-editorial reasons. (When Google wants to appease China, what will happen to GBS books critical of the Chinese government?)

The settlement would also erode fair use and first sale rights. Access to GBS books at public access terminals might be free, but printing out pages would require paying a tax to the BRR, even though photocopying those same pages from a physical book would be fair use. Although consumers can purchase out-of-print books from GBS, these books, unlike those bought for the Kindle, could only be accessed in the cloud. GBS books cannot be lent or freely annotated in the same way real books can be. I could go on, but you get the point. The devil in this agreement lies in its details, which Courant and other proponents ignore.

UNFAIRNESS TO CLASS MEMBERS

Foreign rights holders would be seriously harmed if the October 2008 settlement were approved as is, so it is no wonder that the governments of France and Germany, as well as dozens of publishers from Denmark, the Netherlands, Sweden, Japan, and New Zealand, are among the hundreds of objectors to the settlement.

Among their most serious concerns is that the settlement would give Google the right to make unilateral determinations about whether a book is in or out of print by looking at various U.S.-based information resources. If Google concludes that a book is out of print, it would automatically have the right to commercialize the book by selling ads against its contents, selling individual copies, and including the book in institutional subscriptions. Google would keep 37 percent of these revenues for itself. If foreign rights holders wished to contest an out-of-print determination or ask Google not to commercialize the book, they would have to provide significant documentation to accomplish these objectives. Courant is right that the settlement eases transaction costs for Google, but it imposes significant transaction costs on rights holders, especially on foreigners.

Consider also that if foreign rights holders want to share in GBS revenues generated by their books, they must sign up either as a Google partner or with the BRR, get a U.S. tax ID number, and pay U.S. taxes on Google's commercialization of their books. This may not be a significant hardship for big publishers like Bertelsmann, but for individual author rights holders, it may be very burdensome. One Australian objector estimated that it would cost almost $300 to get a

U.S. tax ID in order to qualify for the $60 payout available from the BRR for the scanning of an Australian author's book.

Nor are serious hardships imposed only on foreign rights holders. Small and specialized American publishers, as well as hundreds of individual American authors—including Harold Bloom and Jonathan Lethem—objected to the settlement as unfair to them. Google has misclassified some of their books as out of print, and they feel burdened by the paperwork that must be undertaken to overcome Google's default settings. Some authors object also to the loss of control over their books and worry about how their books would be presented online (e.g., what kinds of ads would run alongside their texts?). Some also worry that the BRR would spend a high proportion of the income from Google on its own operations, leaving little to pay out to rights holders.

Consider also that Google has the right to negotiate future revenue models with the BRR. Suppose Google decided it wanted to license translations of out-of-print books or make translations with its automatic translation tools. There is nothing in the settlement agreement to stop Google from doing this, or even licensing motion picture versions of GBS books, as long as the BRR agrees.

Other victims of the October 2008 settlement agreement include those who own rights in "orphan" books," that is, books whose copyright owner cannot be found through a reasonably diligent search. The settlement directs the BRR to hold onto orphan book revenues for five years, after which the BRR would pay the monies to registered rights holders, a pure windfall for them. The DOJ observed that this would create a conflict of interest between registered and unregistered rights holders, contravening basic norms of class action lawsuits: that all members of the class must be treated fairly. Several states claim that this windfall payment scheme is inconsistent with their unclaimed funds laws.

CONCLUSION

The October 2008 proposed GBS settlement agreement was withdrawn a week after the DOJ recommended against its approval. An amended agreement was filed with the court in November 2009. Judge Denny Chin held a hearing about the fairness of the amended settlement in February 2010 and rejected the settlement as unfair to the class in March 2011.

At the core of Judge Chin's rejection of the GBS settlement was his concern about whether the class action settlement process could be used to achieve such a massive restructuring of the market for digital books as the GBS deal would bring about. Typically such settlements resolve only the specific dispute between the parties after the judge has assessed the merits of the lawsuit and determined that the class representatives and their lawyers adequately represented the interests of the class as a whole. The broader the settlement's scope, the greater the size of the class, the more forward-looking are its terms, and the more the agreement releases the defendant from liability for future conduct, especially conduct different in kind from the issue in litigation, the less likely it is that a judge will or should approve it. The GBS deal was troublesome on all of these grounds, and Judge Chin thought that the parties should be seeking a legislative, not a judicial, blessing for it.

Come to think of it, Courant may be right in perceiving that Google was trying to work some magic with the GBS deal: if we all concentrated intensely on the immediate public access benefits of the deal, maybe we would be distracted enough not to notice the sleight of hand in the background.

NOTES

1. U.S. Department of Justice, "Statement of Interest Regarding the Proposed Settlement," *Authors Guild, Inc. v. Google, Inc.,* available at

http://thepublicindex.org/docs/letters/usa.pdf. (Case 1:05-cv-08136-DC Document 720. Filed 9/18/2009.)

2. Pamela Samuelson, "Letter to Judge Denny Chin, on Behalf of Academic Author Objectors to the Google Book Search Settlement," *Authors Guild, Inc. v. Google, Inc.*, available at http://thepublicindex.org /docs/letters/samuelson.pdf. (Case1:05-cv-08136-DC. Filed 9/3/2009.)

REFERENCES AND FURTHER READING

Bettanin, Donica. 2009. "Letter to Judge Denny Chin." *Authors Guild, Inc. v. Google, Inc.* Available at http://docs.justia.com/cases/federal /district-courts/newyork/nysdce/1:2005cv08136/273913/674. (Case 1:05-cv-08136-DC Document 674. Filed 9/11/2009.)

Brin, Sergey. 2009. "A Library to Last Forever." *New York Times*, October 9. Available at www.nytimes.com/2009/10/09/opinion/09brin .html.

Courant, Paul. 2009. "The Stakes in the Google Book Search Settlement." *The Economists' Voice* 6, no. 9: art. 7. Available at www.bepress .com/ev/vol6/iss9/art7.

Edlin, Aaron S., and Daniel L. Rubinfeld. 2004. "Exclusion or Efficient Pricing: The 'Big Deal' Bundling of Academic Journals." *Antitrust Law Journal* 7, no. 1. Available at http://works.bepress.com/aaron _edlin/37.

Nunberg, Geoffrey. 2009. "Google's Book Search: A Disaster for Scholars." *Chronicle of Higher Education*, August 31. Available at http:// chronicle.com/article/Googles-Book-Search-A/48245.

Samuelson, Pamela. 2009. "Letter to Judge Denny Chin, on Behalf of Academic Author Objectors to the Google Book Search Settlement." *Authors Guild, Inc. v. Google, Inc.* Available at http://thepublicindex.org /docs/letters/samuelson.pdf. (Case 1:05-cv-08136-DC. Filed 9/3/2009.)

U.S. Department of Justice. 2009. "Statement of Interest Regarding the Proposed Settlement." *Authors Guild, Inc. v. Google, Inc.* Available at http://thepublicindex.org/docs/letters/usa.pdf. (Case 1:05-cv-08136-DC Document 720. Filed 9/18/2009.)

CHAPTER 31

The Stakes in the Google
Book Search Settlement

Paul N. Courant

IN 2004 GOOGLE embarked on a project of historic scope. Its aim was to scan and index the contents of the world's great research libraries. There was one small problem: authors and publishers of works in copyright sued, arguing that Google violated copyright law by scanning works without the explicit permission of rights holders. In the way of most commercial lawsuits, the parties settled, but unlike most commercial lawsuits, the settlement greatly expanded the stakes, creating a great electronic bookstore where Google would sell (with most of the revenue going to rights holders) access to millions of copyrighted works, something not contemplated in Google's original scanning project. The settlement engendered many howls of protest

Paul N. Courant is the Harold T. Shapiro Collegiate Professor of Public Policy and the Arthur F. Thurnau Professor of Economics and of Information at the University of Michigan. He is also the University Librarian and Dean of Libraries and was Provost at Michigan when Google negotiated its original arrangement to digitize the University's collections. This chapter was published in 2009, shortly before the Google Settlement was presented to the Court.

and some expressions of support. Pamela Samuelson (2009), among the most eloquent of the objectors, called the proposed settlement "audacious" and argued that it is "designed to give [Google] a compulsory license to all books in copyright throughout the world forever."

In September, weeks before a scheduled fairness hearing that could have led to approval of the settlement by the court, the court asked the parties for an opportunity to revise the settlement agreement in light of concerns raised by the U.S. Department of Justice and hundreds of other objectors. The court has given the parties a November deadline for a revised agreement.

In my opinion, approval of the original settlement would have been vastly preferable to its rejection, because it provided extraordinary and valuable benefits to readers and scholars. But, in at least one important feature, I believe that the Department of Justice may be pointing the way to a settlement that would be better than the original. Before I come to these conclusions, some background is required.

COPYRIGHT AND THE GOOGLE SCANNING PROJECT

Article I, Section 8, of the United States Constitution gives Congress the power to "promote the progress of science and useful arts, by securing for limited times to authors and inventors the exclusive right to their respective writings and discoveries." The framers struck a classic balance in public economics. They recognized simultaneously that the incentive to develop new knowledge would be enhanced if writers and inventors could capture some of the return on their work (hence, the "exclusive" rights, which are not completely exclusive, with good reason). At the same time, they recognized that knowledge and new discoveries are nonrival, meaning that added users do not diminish the uses of existing users (hence, the free use after "limited times").

Congress has repeatedly extended the "limited time" that is covered by copyright, with the result that most works written in the twentieth century are protected by copyright and unavailable to be read online, even when a perfectly readable scanned copy exists. In brief, what's at stake in the Google Book settlement is our ability to find and read the literature of (most of) the twentieth century online.

Of course, the great majority of works written in the twentieth century are out of print, and most have been out of print since shortly after their publication.

Until Google began its mass digitization of research library collections, access to out-of-print works generally required visiting a library that had a copy. As the digitization project has proceeded (well over twelve million books have been digitized and indexed by Google, with tens of thousands being added every week), an interesting and instructive bifurcation has occurred.

Digitized works known to be in the public domain—including essentially everything published in the United States before 1923 and many works published between 1923 and 1963—are easily available. They can be found through Google Book Search (books.google.com) and on the websites of many participating libraries. They can be read online or downloaded, and in the past several months hundreds of thousands have been made commercially available through a variety of print-on-demand channels, as well as on e-book readers. However, works that may still be in copyright are not so easy to find and to use. Google shows only a brief snippet in response to an online search, along with information about where a physical copy of the book might be found. The reason for the restricted usability of these works is simple: the penalties for displaying significant portions of copyrighted material can be severe—from $750 to $150,000 (no, that's not a typo; there are four zeros after the fifteen) per violation, and each Internet hit would constitute a violation. This is a risk that neither Google nor any library is willing to take.

As result, most of the scholarly and cultural record of the twentieth century cannot be accessed by the methods preferred by pretty much everyone who reads in the twenty-first century. A professor wanting to assign a substantial portion of a book written in, say, 1961 (and out of print for forty-seven years) is generally still required to put the book on reserve the old-fashioned way, even if the university library has a digitized copy that could be put on a server and delivered to students at zero marginal cost.

I have referred to books published after 1922 as books that "may be" in copyright. The copyright law is nothing if not complicated, and among its interesting features is that the current copyright status of books depends on dates of authorship and in many cases on the details of registration and renewal of copyright. To complicate matters further, for many books (the number is surely over half a million in the United States, in the millions worldwide) the holder of copyright is not known and may not exist, and often neither a living author nor a still-extant publisher knows who holds the rights to a given work. Such works are generally referred to as "orphan works" in the world of libraries and copyright lawyers, but they are really a particular kind of orphan—foundlings. Their parents (holders of copyrights in them) are unknown. The existence of orphan works of this kind greatly complicates the already complicated and often expensive effort involved in finding rights holders and making arrangements with them for lawful use of copyrighted works.

THE LAWSUIT AND PROPOSED SETTLEMENT

Google announced its mass digitization project with libraries in 2004. In 2005 several authors and publishers of copyrighted works, respectively working with the Authors Guild and the Association of American Publishers, sued Google for unauthorized copying of copyrighted works. Google's defense was to argue that its indexing of the works and displaying of snippets constituted a fair use under the copyright law. Some three years later, the parties to the suit agreed to a settlement, with the plaintiffs claiming to represent a class that includes essentially all those who hold copyright to works in libraries in the United States. The settlement agreement cannot go into effect without Federal District Court approval and is currently under revision as a result of concerns that have been vigorously expressed by many parties, including the Department of Justice.

Basically the proposed settlement would create a market in electronically available copies of out-of-print works that are plausibly in copyright. Google would provide free browsing access (usually 20 percent of a book would be viewable in a given search) and would sell permanent online access to complete versions on behalf of itself and a newly created Book Rights Registry (BRR) that would represent the interests of rights holders of works subject to the settlement. Google would also sell site licenses to institutions such as colleges and universities, enabling students and employees of those institutions to have access to the collections in much the same way that they now have access to electronic journals and databases purchased by their libraries. Google would obtain 37 percent of the revenue from both the retail product and the site license, with the rest to be distributed to rights holders.

The obvious benefit of the settlement is that it provides electronic access to many millions of works at one fell swoop, saving the transactions costs that would be involved if Google, libraries, and others seeking to provide access to the scanned works had to negotiate work by work and rights holder by rights holder, assuming that rights holders could be found. The ability to search simultaneously the collections of the world's great research libraries, to browse those collections, and to be able to purchase immediate electronic access provides uncalculated, but almost certainly large, consumer surplus.

The settlement would also permit academic libraries and their universities, at least after a time, to save a great deal of money and space, as the necessity of holding extensively duplicated print collections would be eliminated. Moreover, the settlement includes the orphan (foundling) works, removing the risks that would otherwise attend to displaying works where rights are unknown and adding to the value that would be available to students, professors, and other users of Google's newly created giant electronic bookstore. Inclusion of the orphan works is essential to creating an effective product for the academic market, because without them neither Google nor anyone else could risk putting collections online without costly establishment of rights (or the lack thereof) book by book, and the resulting collection of out-of-print works would be seriously incomplete. One can never conclusively prove a book to be orphaned. There is always the possibility that a rights holder will materialize, with a lawyer not far behind.

OBJECTIONS

The objections to the original settlement agreement are many and varied. One set involves privacy, which I do not consider here. Others involve a cluster of legal questions, notably involving technical issues of civil procedure surrounding class action lawsuits, of which I have little interest and less understanding. Still others have a good deal of economic content.

The settlement would plausibly bestow considerable market power on the BRR and Google. Although other parties could choose to scan libraries' works and provide market access by contracting with the BRR, only Google would be authorized to use the Google scans in the marketplace, and for at least the foreseeable future, the Google scans constitute the overwhelming majority of scans, because no one else has been willing to commit the hundreds of millions of dollars necessary to scan the tens of millions of works that reside in the world's research libraries.

Many objections to the Google settlement are based on a concern that Google and the BRR will have monopoly power in the newly developed market for electronic access to out-of-print copyrighted works. Some assertions in this regard are simply silly: Google will not have a monopoly on access to the works, which are still available in the source libraries. Nor will it have been granted a monopoly on electronic access to works with known rights holders; such works may be rescanned and sold by other providers, including rights holders themselves, should it prove to be the case that the market in these works is sufficiently profitable to attract entry.

The orphan works are another matter. The settlement gives Google rights to distribute orphan works and provides for no mechanism that could practically convey such rights to other entities. Moreover, unlike the situation when rights holders are known, there is no way for copyright holders of orphaned works to contract with other parties for distribution of those works, because it is in the nature of orphan works that the holders of the rights are unknown. This leads the Department of Justice to be concerned that the settlement, as drafted, "appears to create a dangerous probability that only Google would have the ability to market to libraries and other institutions a comprehensive digital-book subscription" (U.S. Department of Justice 2009, 24).

EXPLOITING THE ORPHANS

The disposition of both the orphan works and revenues attributed to them is one of the most controversial features of the settlement. One important economic objection is distributional. There is clear public benefit to providing access to orphan works. But under the settlement agreement, if the rights holders to orphan works are not found after five years, the principal beneficiaries of the revenues attributable to orphan works would be the authors and publishers who hold the rights to *other* works. Why them? Well, to be honest, one can't help but think that it is because these rights holders were active parties in the lawsuits, whereas orphans, parents, consumers, and others were not. Other obvious possibilities would be to return these funds to consumers as rebates, to give them to the libraries that bought and preserved the works in the first place (would I have thought of this were I not Michigan's librarian?), or to reduce the federal deficit.

That Google has an advantageous position with regard to the orphan works is clear. Whether that position is worth any money to speak of is an open question. Books that are in copyright and out of print have already proved themselves to be something less than star performers in the marketplace. To be sure, libraries will find it valuable to have access to as complete a collection as possible. At the same time, the settlement adduces a principle of "broad access" in determining prices for institutional licenses. Moreover, the orphan works will continue to be available in print form and as part of Google's retail product, and 20 percent of each book will be available for free preview. Additionally, it seems likely that Google is more interested in attracting people to its site than it is in profiting directly from sales of books, and hence it would prefer prices to be low.

Sadly, I don't have an estimate of the price elasticity of demand for out-of-print works with unknown owners, but I am confident that Google's ability to exploit its monopoly position in orphan works is far weaker than the ability of commercial journal publishers to exploit their position in fields where getting the next essential grant requires immediate access to the most current published papers. The fear among some librarians, including Robert Darnton of Harvard (2009), that Google will be able to set extortionate prices in the manner of many commercial journal publishers (not including bepress), seems to me to misapprehend important differences between old books and current scientific journal articles. Professor Darnton and I have debated the question at some length in a recent exchange in *The New York Review of Books*.

Fortunately, concerns about legal barriers to entry can be laid to rest by changing the treatment of the orphan works while preserving the benefits of the settlement to the public and to the scholarly community. All of the efficiency gains from the settlement's treatment of orphan works are due to the settlement's waiver of legal liability from their sale and display. That waiver makes the books available and generates value for those who would search and read them. The distribution of revenues to rights holders of other books serves no compelling distributional interest.

Thus any mechanisms that allowed other entities (e.g., libraries, publishers, the Internet Archive, Microsoft) to display and facilitate the search of orphan works on the same or similar terms that Google has under the draft settlement would realize the efficiency gains without distributional harm. And by allowing entry, any such mechanism would eliminate the most troubling element of a potential monopoly that could arise from the settlement.

Thus a revised settlement (as suggested by the U.S. Department of Justice 2009, 25) that provided competitors with the ability to use the orphan works on the same terms as Google, or legislation with a similar consequence, would be an unambiguous improvement over the original settlement. The great benefit of a new market in electronic versions of the literature of most of the twentieth century could be realized with a reduced risk of monopoly and without enriching unrelated parties with the fruits of orphans' labor. In contrast, scuttling of the settlement or greatly limiting the volume of works to be covered would put us back to where we started—the only people with good access to the scholarly and cultural record of the twentieth century would be those with physical access to research libraries, and even for them, that literature would be more difficult to access than most works published before or since.

REFERENCES AND FURTHER READING

American Library Association. Available at http://wo.ala.org/gbs. (The Google Book Search Settlement website has many of the basic documents and a good deal of commentary, including a list of parties that filed comments with the court.)

Band, Jonathan. 2008. "A Guide for the Perplexed: Libraries and the Google Library Project Settlement." Association of Research Libraries. Available at http://wo.ala.org/gbs/alaarl-summary-document. (A link to the settlement itself can be found at the same URL.)

Darnton, Robert. 2009. "Google and the Future of Books." *New York Review of Books* 56, no. 2 (February 12). Available at www.nybooks.com/articles/22281. (See also Paul Courant's response and Darnton's rejoinder, available at www.nybooks.com/articles/22496.)

Samuelson, Pamela. 2009. "The Audacity of the Google Book Settlement." *The Huffington Post*, August 10. Available at www.huffingtonpost.com/pamela-samuelson/the-audacityof-the-googl_b_255490.html. (Also see links to other commentary by Professor Samuelson.)

U.S. Department of Justice. 2009. "Justice Department Submits Views on Proposed Google Book Search Settlement." Available at www.usdoj.gov/opa/pr/2009/September/09-opa-1001.html. (Case 1:05-cv-08136-DC Document 720. Filed 09/18/2009.)

CHAPTER 32

The NFL Should Auction Possession in Overtime Games

Yeon-Koo Che and Terrence Hendershott

SUPER BOWL XLIII of 2009 featured one of the closest contests in Super Bowl history. If not for the miraculous catch by Santonio Holmes in the waning seconds, the Steelers might have kicked a game-tying field goal and the Super Bowl would have gone into overtime.

In a sense, however, overtimes can ruin great games, because, with all too high probability, whichever team gets the ball first wins. Instead of one of the best, the game might have been remembered as dubious, maybe even ignominious, with many "what ifs." We propose an auction method to eliminate the coin flip's randomness by letting the teams bid to determine the initial possession.

Yeon-Koo Che is the Kelvin J. Lancaster Professor of Economic Theory in the Economics Department at Columbia University. Terrence Hendershott is a tenured Associate Professor at Haas School of Business, University of California, Berkeley.

WHY THE CURRENT OVERTIME PROCESS STINKS

Suppose that at the end of tie games, the referee simply flipped a coin to determine who won. Everyone would scream that this was unfair, or, if unfair is the wrong word, it would certainly be silly. What would be the point of calling this winning?

And yet what happens is not so far from that. From 2000 through 2007, in 37 of the 124 overtime games, the team that won the initial coin toss won on its initial possession. Could overtime outcomes be made more "fair"—by which we mean, could randomness be reduced to increase the role skill and execution play in determining the outcome?

DIAGNOSING THE PROBLEM

Part of the issue with the current NFL overtime rule is its sudden death format; namely, that an overtime game is won by the first team to score. Sudden death, however, keeps the playing time manageable in light of the physical nature of the sport and the network's broadcasting constraints. Also, sudden death is not unfair by itself, as before the coin flip neither team has an advantage. It is only unfair to the extent that the possession, or receiving an opening kickoff, confers a significant advantage, as it now does.

A clue to the nature of the problem and to its solution is found by asking what happened in 1994. That year, the NFL moved the kickoff spot from the 35- to the 30-yard line, where it remains today, which ensures that the receiving team gets a good field position. Field position is everything, as any watcher of football knows, and as David Romer (2006) has extensively documented.

ECONOMICS (BUT NOT ECONOMISTS) TO THE RESCUE

One lesson of economics is that markets or auctions produce fairer and less random outcomes. To minimize the impact of luck, it must be the case that the team that receives the opening possession has no real advantage. To accomplish this, *why not let the teams trade on who receives the opening possession with the starting position used as currency?*

Although the idea is an economic one, it came first from those who care about the problem most—not from economists. Chris Quanbeck, an electrical engineer and a Green Bay Packers fan, was the first to suggest the idea of auctioning off the possession, according to an article in *Slate*. According to his idea, the team offering to start at a position closest to one's own end line would win possession at that position.

How can opening a market help make the overtime game less random and, therefore, more fair? Imagine that you offered each team the chance to have the first possession 100 yards from its own goal, ready to score. Each would grab at the chance, so it wouldn't be fair to give it to either. What about 90 yards? Well, again, both teams would want the ball. On the other hand, neither would want the ball backed up against its own goal. So is there a distance $x^\star$ in between where it wouldn't matter to either team, whether A started with the ball $x^\star$ yards from its goal line or B started with the ball $x^\star$ yards from its goal line? Typically, there will be, as illustrated in Figure 32.1.

Say team A will win with probability $p(x)$ against team B if A has possession x yards from A's goal line, and with probability $q(x)$ if B has possession x yards from B's goal line; $p(x)$ is the upward sloping line and $q(x)$ is the downward sloping line in Figure 32.1. As x rises, $p(x)$ will go up because it gets easier for A to score, at least from a field goal, as one gets close to the other team's end line. Likewise, $q(x)$ will fall with x because B too is more likely to win the farther from its own goal line it takes possession, which makes A less likely to win.

FIGURE 32.1

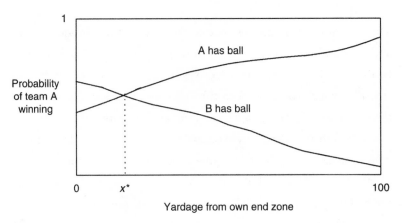

Consider the x★ that equates p and q, the x★ such that p(x★) = q(x★). Both teams must be indifferent to possession at x★. For example, it might be that the Steelers are just as likely to win if they get the ball at their own 18-yard line as if the Cardinals get the ball at the 18-yard line, that is, p(18) = q(18). But then the Cardinals should be indifferent to possession at precisely 18 yards, since 1 − q(18) = 1 − p(18).

But how would we find such an x★? Easy. Hold an auction.

Consider an auction in which each team is bidding for possession of the ball. The auction is descending in field position, which means that x begins at 100 yards, which means taking the ball at 100 yards from one's own goal line. Each team would love that opportunity! Teams successively bid lower numbers, x, in an attempt to win the auction and get to start with the ball x yards from their own goal line. The lowest bid wins.

Suppose that the current bid is at x and team A is more likely to win if it starts with the ball x yards from its goal line than if B starts with the ball x yards from B's goal line: that is p(x) > q(x). For such an x, A will lower its bid. Remarkably, team B will also want to lower its bid as well because 1 − q(x) > 1 − p(x), and 1 − q(x) is the probability that B wins if B takes the ball x yards from B's goal line, and 1 − p(x) is the probability that B wins if A takes the ball at x yards from A's goal line. Thus bids will go down until x falls to x*.

In fact, any standard auction could be used to achieve the same result. The point is that the auctions will force the teams to bid so that opening possession yields no real advantage. This outcome increases fairness by eliminating the randomness of the coin flip: the team losing possession at the bid of x* does not envy that possession. Further, if two teams are equally strong or skilled, as is likely given the game is going into overtime, then they will win with the same likelihood; that is, if $p(x) = 1 - q(x)$ for all x, then $p(x^*) = q(x^*) = \frac{1}{2}$.

Instead of an auction, one could apply another classical idea, namely, the "divide-and-choose" method, to achieve the same outcome. One team (divider), selected by, say, coin flipping, proposes "x" and the other team (chooser) chooses between gaining and ceding possession at the chosen x. Say team A is the divider. Then, fearing that team B will choose the bigger of $1 - p(x)$ and $1 - q(x)$, thus leaving it with the "shorter end of the stick," team A will equalize $p(x)$ and $q(x)$ by proposing x*.

COMPLICATIONS

The aforementioned theory is all very elegant, but it is unlikely that the teams will have a common and accurate understanding of the probabilities of each team winning starting at each position, as we have implicitly assumed. Each team presumably knows more than its opponent about the status of its own offense and defense units and, more importantly, its own kickers at the start of overtime. We (see Che and Hendershott 2008) argue in a paper in *Economics Letters* that in such a realistic setting, auctioning off the possession is fairer than divide and choose.

Suppose, for instance, that each team "guesses" x* with some error and that two teams' guesses combined are more accurate than one team's guess. In divide and choose, the divider will likely propose his best guess on $x^\star$, and this may "tip off" his information. The chooser may exploit this by acting on even better information than either team has. This means that coin flipping is again necessary to settle the imbalance, which brings us full circle.

Auctions avoid coin flipping altogether, since they treat both teams symmetrically. Standard ascending or descending auctions as well as sealed-bid auctions have this property and will do as well in aggregating guesses. They may engender strategic reactions, however. A winner's (low bidder's) guess on $x^\star$ is likely biased below, and the loser's guess is likely biased above, true $x^\star$. So teams may adjust their bids upward to overcome the "winner's curse" in an ascending or first-price (low-bid) sealed-bid auction and adjust their bids downward to overcome "loser's curse" in a descending or second-price (high-bid) auction. Such strategic reactions and possible mistakes can be minimized if the starting position is determined in a sealed-bid auction by the *average of the low and high bids*—our favorite proposal. To the extent that the best combined guess is close to the average of each team's guess—a reasonable guess—each team will not gain much from strategizing and will be protected from possible mistakes in this format.

WHY NOT?

The NFL is aware of current overtime rules' shortcomings. Prior to Super Bowl XLIII, NFL commissioner Roger Goodell suggested a new overtime format in which the team that takes the opening kickoff cannot win by a field goal on its first possession. While this would eliminate the most egregious overtime outcome, any proposal that does not take into consideration the teams and field conditions cannot fully eliminate the impact of the coin flip. The auction eliminates the coin flip and enables the teams to account for all relevant information.

Implementing an auction to begin the overtime would be a daring move for the NFL, but, as Tim Harford (2009) points out, it could be very entertaining. Imagine the opportunities for fans and commentators to second-guess coaches' bidding strategies, saying things like, "Boy, I would have thought the Raiders would be more aggressive than that in their bidding given how well their offense is doing. One way to look at it is they are showing confidence in their defense, but given the number of points the Dolphins have scored today, that seems crazy."

REFERENCES AND FURTHER READING

Che, Y.-K., and T. Hendershott. 2008. "How to Divide the Possession of a Football?" *Economics Letters* 99, no. 3: 561–65. Available at http://works.bepress.com/yeonkoo/15.

Harford, Tim. 2009. "Flipping Awful: Why the NFL Should Replace the Overtime Coin Toss with an Auction System." *Slate Magazine*, January 29. Available at www.slate.com/id/2209436.

Romer, David. 2006. "Do Firms Maximize? Evidence from Professional Football." *Journal of Political Economy* 114, no. 2: 340–65. Available at http://elsa.berkeley.edu/~dromer/papers/JPE_April06.pdf.

Index